To Be A Pilot

6th Edition

Edited by Ian Penberthy

Airlife

First edition published in 1982 by
Airlife Publishing, an imprint of
The Crowood Press Ltd
Ramsbury, Marlborough
Wiltshire SN8 2HR

www.crowood.com

Sixth edition 2008

British Library Cataloguing-in-Publication Data
A catalogue record for this book is available from the British Library.

ISBN 978 1 84797 013 8

Disclaimer
The information contained in this book is believed to be correct at
the time of publication. However, the author and publishers cannot
be held responsible or liable for action taken on this information.
Terms, details and conditions are constantly subject to change by the
relevant authorities. All material relating to the Private Pilot Licence,
National Private Pilot Licence, Commercial Pilot Licence, Airline
Transport Pilot Licence and associated ratings should be checked
against the Civil Aviation Authority publication *LASORS*.

Page 2: The Cirrus SR20 is one of a new breed of composite
private aircraft. It has digital instrumentation and a ballistic recovery
parachute that can be deployed in an emergency to lower the aircraft
safely to the ground. (Adrian Pingstone)

Printed and bound in Singapore by Craft P

CONTENTS

Foreword by HRH Prince Philip, Duke of Edinburgh   6

Introduction and Acknowledgements   7

Chapter 1   About Aircraft   9

Chapter 2   The Private Pilot Licence   19

Chapter 3   The National Private Pilot Licence   51

Chapter 4   The Commercial Pilot   57

Chapter 5   The Military Pilot   84

Chapter 6   Contact Names and Addresses   106

List of Abbreviations   152

Index   154

There is no accounting for taste and there is even less accounting for the choice of occupation. Some people may develop a burning ambition to fly at a very early age, others may find it unappealing at best and positively frightening at worst. Unfortunately, ambition does not necessarily go with aptitude. Lucky are the people who find that they have a natural aptitude for the one thing they desperately want to do.

In theory, flying an aeroplane is no more difficult than driving a car. In practice flying an aeroplane is more like steering a boat. A car is, or should be, permanently connected to a road; aircraft and boats operate in the fluid media where the condition of the weather is a far more critical factor for a pilot than for a driver.

For anyone with the ambition, or the obsession, to take up any occupation, it is always a good idea to find out as much about it as possible before becoming too committed. This book is designed precisely for this purpose. Having read it, I think it is worth your while to bear in mind that a flying career is much more than just a meal-ticket with fringe benefits. You will find an endless challenge in all aeronautical matters; that you are constantly having to cope with new equipment, new techniques and new concepts. Most important of all, you will find that you have got to keep on top of a flying job both for your own peace of mind as well as for the safety of the people who put themselves in your care.

Foreword from the First Edition

INTRODUCTION

'Don't envy the birds, join them! If you can drive a car, you can fly an aircraft!' Popular lines quoted encouragingly in the advertisements of light aircraft manufacturers and flying schools. You have probably seen them, and perhaps wondered if it can possibly be true. Can anyone fly? Could *you* do it?

The answer is a qualified 'yes'. Just about anyone can be taught to handle the controls of an aircraft. Young children have done it, and so have elderly grandparents. In truth, however, the most commonly quoted parallel, that between driving and flying, is not really a valid comparison. Flying an aircraft can actually be easier than driving a car. There is much less traffic to worry about for one thing. Nevertheless, flying does demand quite different skills, and levels of skill, to those required of the motorist. A pilot needs a co-ordination of mind, hand and eye that quite simply is not an inherent part of everyone's make-up. Just as a few people are 'natural' drivers or sports players, so many struggle to master even the rudiments, and some never do.

To put it very simply, a pilot needs a good car driver's co-ordination and reflexes, a horse rider's sense of balance and subtle touch of hand, a sailor's eye for weather, and much else besides. It is possible to teach almost anyone the basic mechanical ability to control an aircraft in flight, but not everyone can hone that skill to the level necessary to become a safe and proficient pilot.

Lots of words and phrases in aviation tend to be abbreviated. Therefore, this book contains many such instances. To assist the reader, and to avoid the need to read back through sections of text, a full glossary of abbreviations is provided on page 152.

This is not intended to be a textbook for those wishing to learn how to fly. There are many excellent training manuals on the market that deal with the subject. This book's purpose is to whet the appetites of aspiring private and professional fliers, and to help answer those questions: **'Could I do it? Could I fly? Do I have what it takes to be a pilot?'**

ACKNOWLEDGEMENTS

For their help in supplying information for Mike Jerram's first, second and third editions of *To Be A Pilot*, thanks go to Air Cdre C.A. Aldose CB DEC AFC MA, secretary to The Air League Educational Trust; the British Air Line Pilots Association; Capt Graham Jenkins, former manager of Flight Crew Resourcing at British Airways; the Flight Crew Licensing and Information and Publicity departments of the Civil Aviation Authority; Danny Forman MBE, chief executive of the General Aviation Manufacturers & Traders Association; Miss Hazel Prosper, Corps Director of the Girls Venture Corps; Jack Nicholl, Peter Latham and Colin Beckwith, past principals of Oxford Air Training School; James Gilbert, editor of *Pilot*, for permission to adapt certain material that first appeared in the magazine; Flt Lt Larry Chamberlain of HQ Air Cadets, RAF Newton; Sqn Ldr G.L. Margitta BA RAF, Royal Air Force College, Cranwell; the staffs of the Army, Royal Air Force and Royal Navy Careers Offices; and the public relations staff of British Airways, British Aerospace, and RAF Strike and Support Commands.

For their assistance in producing the amendments and additions for the fourth and fifth editions, thanks go to Bob Fielding (Lt RN Retired); Lt Cdr P.J. Hardy RN; Pauline Harris, Brian Marindin, CFI, and CPL/IR instructors at Airways Flight Training, Exeter; Chris Martin; Julia Hines of the Cabair Group; Scott Brown, FAA Gatwick; Peter Moxhan, marketing manager, Oxford Air Training School; Mike Beeston, CFI, Exeter Air Training School; Maj (Retired) R.A. James MBE, Headquarters, Director Army Aviation, Middle Wallop; Tony Hines, Aviation Training Association; Public Relations Office, HQ Air Cadets, RAF Newton; Wg Cdr Alan Watson and Sqn Ldr David Cuthbertson, Headquarters University Air Squadrons, Royal Air Force College, Cranwell; David Snelling of the British Airways press office; Minesh Patel of the British Airways Flight Operations Training Centre, Heathrow; Captain Peter McKellar, CAA Examiner.

For their advice and assistance in producing this latest edition of *To Be A Pilot*, thanks must go to Marc Cornelius of 80:20 PR Limited; Pia Berqvist of Cessna Corporate Communications; Loretta Conley of the Robinson Helicopter Company; Steve Willmot of the Ministry of Defence; Kenneth Hall of JK Aviation; and the staff of Sussex Flying Club.

CHAPTER 1
ABOUT AIRCRAFT

Whatever your eventual aim in aviation – to fly simply for pleasure as a private pilot, to become an airline pilot or even a fighter pilot – your basic tool will be the same: an aircraft. Every would-be flier's introduction to flying is likely to be in a small training aircraft.

Most flying schools in Britain use American aircraft. The types most likely to be encountered at any typical flying school are the high-wing Cessna 152 and Aerobat, and the low-wing Piper Tomahawk, Cherokee, Cadet and Warrior. All are similar in concept, being two- or four-seaters with side-by-side seating, fixed tricycle undercarriages (with a nosewheel at the front) and four-cylinder, air-cooled, horizontally opposed piston engines in the 100–180hp range. There are a few flying schools that operate tailwheel aircraft for training and, should you wish, it is still possible to learn to fly in a vintage open-cockpit aircraft such as the de Havilland Tiger Moth, which first began training pilots in the 1930s.

Let us look at one of the most common training aircraft, the venerable Cessna 152. Introduced in 1977, this machine continues to perform sterling service in many flying schools. Although its high-wing layout is not to

The Cessna 150/152 series has been training pilots for decades. The high-wing layout provides stability in flight because the fuselage acts like a pendulum. It also offers a good downward view, but restricts upward vision.

For those who want to pursue a more traditional training route, it is still possible to learn on older types of aircraft, such as the de Havilland Tiger Moth, although modern types have to be employed for instrument flying.

everyone's taste, because the wings restrict the pilot's vision overhead and when turning, the design provides good visibility in a downward direction and also contributes to stability in flight. Conversely, in a low-wing type such as the Piper Warrior, upward visibility is less restricted but the wings obscure a substantial part of the downward view. Low-wing aircraft with large clear canopies, such as the French Robin 200 and 400, and German Grob 115, provide the best compromise, but it is still a case of 'swings and roundabouts'. Each type has its champions. In common with all conventional aircraft, the Cessna 152's airframe comprises three primary elements: the fuselage, which contains the cockpit or cabin area; an engine, in this case a 108hp Textron-Lycoming O-235 mounted at the front of the fuselage; and

Most light aircraft have air-cooled, horizontally opposed engines of either four or six cylinders. This example is a Lycoming O-235, the same type as fitted to the Cessna 152. (A. Hunt)

The Piper PA-28 Cherokee's low-wing layout makes for a less claustrophobic feeling in the cabin, but does hide a significant amount of the ground. Unlike the Cessna 150/152, it is a four-seater. (Adrian Pingstone)

flying surfaces – the wings and tail group. These, in turn, have movable control surfaces that, when used in various combinations, direct the movement of the aircraft in the air.

CONTROL SURFACES

The Tail Group

Normally, there is a fixed horizontal surface known as the tailplane or, in US parlance, the horizontal stabilizer. Two movable panels are attached to the rear edge of the tailplane by means of hinges, and are known as elevators. Some aircraft have tailplanes that move in their entirety, popularly called 'stabilators'. The elevators (or stabilators) control the aircraft in the pitch axis. Imagine the aircraft from the side (profile) view. Its centre of gravity (cg) is roughly at a point one-quarter to one-third back from the leading (forward) edge of the wing. Now imagine an axis or shaft passing through that point from wingtip to wingtip. In pitch, the aircraft will pivot about that axis, nose-up or nose-down, and the hinged elevators control the direction of that movement. When the pilot raises the elevators using the control wheel or stick, a downward force is created on the aircraft's tail in flight, thus raising the nose, and vice versa. Set into one elevator is a smaller hinged surface called a trim tab. Its function is to relieve the pilot of the control force needed to hold the elevators at any desired angle, to trim the aircraft at a selected pitch angle. It is adjusted by a small wheel or handle in the cockpit, moving in the opposite direction to the desired elevator movement: trim tab down, elevator up; trim tab up, elevator down.

The fixed vertical tail surface is called a fin, or vertical stabilizer in US

11

The aircraft's tail group comprises the vertical fin and rudder, and the horizontal tailplane and elevators. A small hinged flap in the trailing edge of one of the elevators is used to trim the setting, thus relieving the pilot of the need to apply a lot of force to the controls to maintain it.

parlance. Its rakish angle or sweepback is more for reasons of styling than for aerodynamic purposes. The hinged rear surface of the fin is the rudder, the function of which is to control the aircraft in its yaw or normal axis. Let us return to our cg point, but this time imagine the aircraft in plan view, as seen from directly above, with the axis or shaft passing vertically through the cg. Now imagine the nose of the aircraft swinging from side to side as it revolves around the axis. That is yaw, and it is controlled by the rudder, which is moved by a pair of pedals.

The Wings
Set in the trailing (rear) edge at the end of each wing is a narrow hinged surface called an aileron. Unlike the elevators on the tailplane, which move in unison, the ailerons move in opposition. That is, as one goes up, the other goes down. They control the aircraft in its roll axis. In this case, the axis or shaft passes through the aircraft from nose to tail. Picture the aircraft head-on, in front view, and imagine one wing dipping, rotating the aircraft about the shaft. This is called rolling, or banking, and it is governed by the ailerons through movement of the control wheel or stick.

Inboard from the ailerons are two larger surfaces called flaps. Unlike the elevators and ailerons, flaps cannot be raised above the fixed surface to which they are attached. Instead, they drop down and retract flush with the wing surface. Their purpose is to provide additional lift to the wing by altering the camber (curvature) of its aerofoil surface. They also create drag and act as

Ailerons and flaps are set into the trailing edge of the wing. The ailerons are placed out toward the tip of the wing and are used to bank the aircraft in one direction or the other. The flaps are positioned inboard, being used to increase lift during slow flight or provide drag during a descent to land.

aerodynamic brakes for slow flight or during the landing approach. Flaps can be manually operated through a lever and simple mechanical linkage, as in the Piper PA-28, or electrically activated, like those on the Cessna 152.

THE COCKPIT

In the Cessna 152, there are two seats mounted side-by-side, and the interior is not too generous on room for large-framed occupants. Ahead is the instrument panel, projecting from which are dual control wheels, allowing either occupant to take control. 'Wheel' is something of a misnomer, because they are not round on most modern aircraft, but are shaped like one half of a spectacle frame, or like a flattened letter 'W'; they are often called control yokes. Some training aircraft, usually of European origin, still have a conventional control column rather than a wheel. This is floor-mounted and hinged at its base, a 'joystick' in the old Royal Air Force jargon. However, wheels are much more common. They are mounted on shafts that slide in and out of the instrument panel, while the wheels themselves also rotate, car-style, although over a much more limited 'lock-to-lock' range. They do not steer the aircraft on the ground, however, as most student pilots discover on their first flight, when they turn the wheel energetically and wonder why the aircraft refuses to follow their command.

The control wheel moves the elevators (back for up, forward for down) and the ailerons (wheel to the right to bank right, and vice versa). The rudder is controlled by a pair of pedals mounted in the footwell. Pushing on the left pedal applies left rudder and yaws the aircraft to the left, while right pedal gives right rudder and right yaw. The system is logical, but not entirely natural. At first, many student pilots feel a strong urge to try to slew the aircraft to the left or right as they would a soap-box go-cart, using exactly the opposite of the correct rudder-pedal movement. Normally, the rudder pedals are linked to a steerable nosewheel, which is effective when the aircraft is on the ground. Steering when taking off, landing and taxying is accomplished with the feet, using both rudder and nose-wheel. The rudder pedals may also operate brakes on the aircraft's main wheels, although some trainers have hand-operated brakes; all have a parking brake. On aircraft fitted with toe-brakes, pressure on the top of the rudder pedals operates the brakes, either in unison or individually (to assist in making a tight turn while taxying or parking, for example). They are sensitive and require much lighter pressures than the brake pedals in most family cars.

Remember the trim tab? It is operated by a trim wheel, which may be set in a central console or between the seats, as in the Cessna 152. In some cases, it will take the form of a hand crank set in the cabin roof area, as on some Piper Cherokee models. Trim wheels operate in the natural sense: forward movement of the wheel to trim nose-down, backward movement to trim nose-up. They are marked with a neutral position, at which point the trim tab lies flush with the elevator surface.

OTHER CONTROLS

There is a fuel selector that may have a simple on/off movement to allow the fuel to flow from the tanks in the wings, or it may permit the selection of individual (left/right) tanks as required. In simple high-wing aircraft, such as the Cessna 152, fuel is fed to the engine by that most reliable of forces, gravity, so there are no fuel pumps to concern us. In low-wing types, an electric fuel pump is used to ensure a constant flow of fuel during engine starting, take-off and landing. An engine-driven fuel pump provides a reliable fuel supply in cruising flight.

There are three principal engine controls: the throttle, the mixture control and the carburettor-heat control.

The throttle sets the required power, much like the accelerator pedal in a car, except that when flying, you do not have to make constant adjustments as you might when driving. Once the desired power setting has been selected, it is left until a change in flight configuration, such as a climb or descent, demands a new setting. The throttle is hand operated and can take the form of a simple push-pull knob or a quadrant-mounted 'power lever'. Whichever type the aircraft has (the Cessna 152's throttle is the push-pull type), the throttle control operates in the natural sense: forward to increase power, back to reduce it. A friction nut or collar is provided, which is tightened to hold the power setting required.

The instrument panel of a Cessna 152 – far less daunting than many imagine. Control yokes operate the ailerons and elevators, while pedals control the rudder. The duplication of these controls, plus the central positioning of the throttle and other essential engine controls, allows the aircraft to be flown from either seat, making it an ideal trainer.

The mixture control, readily identified by its red knob, controls the fuel/air mixture reaching the engine. During training flights, usually it will be found in the rich (fully forward) position. Leaning the mixture (reducing the fuel/air ratio) provides greater fuel economy and smoother running at altitude, but this will not concern the student during the earliest training flights. When the mixture control is pulled fully back (out from the instrument panel), it is in the 'idle cut-off' position, and the engine will be starved of fuel and will soon stop. The mixture control is moved to idle cut-off only when the aircraft is on the ground and parked, or during airborne or ground emergencies, when cutting off the flow of fuel to the engine may be necessary – hence the cautionary red knob.

The carburettor heat control takes the form of a push-pull knob or lever. It is used to provide heated air (from a muff around the exhaust pipe) to the carburettor to prevent ice from forming in the carburettor intake. If ice is allowed to develop, a loss of power can result, so heat is applied at regular intervals as a preventive measure. Carburettor icing can occur under certain quite common climatic conditions in the UK, and not only in winter. Unlike the throttle and mixture controls, the carburettor heat control is pulled out to function (hot air) and pushed in to revert to ambient-temperature air.

Supplementary to these primary engine controls, but no less vital, is a

15

magneto switch, marked 'off-left-right-both' for the engine's dual-ignition system: this comprises two separate sets of sparking plugs and their associated wiring, each set being controlled by its own magneto, ensuring that the engine will continue to develop power even if one system fails. Each magneto is tested before flight by selecting first 'right', then 'left', but the 'both' position is used at all other times. The magneto switch usually doubles as a starter switch by turning the aircraft's ignition key past the 'both' position to start, just like a car.

There is a plunger-type primer for priming the aircraft's engine with fuel before starting. Usually, this is necessary only when the engine is cold.

THE INSTRUMENTS

Airliner cockpits have dozens of instruments seemingly spread over every available piece of cockpit wall and roof, although these are increasingly being replaced by electronic flight instrumentation system (EFIS) cathode-ray-tube (CRT) displays in the 'glass cockpits' of new-generation transport aircraft. Such aircraft also have two or three highly trained crew members to monitor their instrument displays. A light training aircraft's instrument array is much more modest.

There are three main types of instrument on the panel: flight instruments, engine and system instruments, and navigation instruments.

Flight Instruments

The flight instruments comprise the airspeed indicator (ASI), altimeter, artificial horizon, vertical speed indicator (VSI), turn-and-slip indicator, and direction indicator (DI). Although it is included in this section on flight instruments, the direction indicator is primarily a navigation instrument that indicates the aircraft's heading in degrees magnetic against a compass card, and does not influence the control of the aircraft.

The airspeed indicator displays the aircraft's speed in miles per hour or knots (nautical miles per hour). That is its speed through the air, not over the ground. The ground speed varies according to whether the aircraft is flying into a headwind or gaining the benefit of a tailwind. The airspeed indicator operates by measuring the static pressure of (still) air surrounding the aircraft and comparing it with the dynamic (moving) pressure of air flowing past the aircraft.

The altimeter also measures air pressure. Essentially, it is an aneroid barometer with an adjustable sub-scale, which is pre-set to a known pressure value. In training, you will soon become acquainted with two common pressure settings, identified by the 'Q' codes QFE and QNH.

The 'Q' codes are a form of abbreviation once commonly used in air-to-ground communications in the days of wireless telegraphy. Today, their use is mostly restricted to aviation and a few other specialized activities. The QFE is the local airfield pressure setting, which will cause the altimeter to read zero when the aircraft is on the ground at that airfield. The QNH is a sea-level pressure setting, which will make the altimeter indicate the airfield's elevation (height above sea level) when the aircraft is on the ground.

Altimeters are calibrated in feet, with the adjustable sub-scale graduated in millibars, inches of mercury or hectopascals. An altimeter works on a pressure differential, giving altitude above sea level (QNH) or above the elevation of the airfield whose local pressure (QFE) has been set. It does not tell you your height above the ground over which you are flying. Consequently, if you fly over a hill that is 1,000ft high with an altimeter reading 1,500ft on the sea-level (QNH) pressure setting, your altitude will be 1,500ft above sea level, but your height (or vertical clearance) above the hill will be only 500ft.

The vertical speed indicator measures the rate of pressure change as the aircraft climbs or descends, and presents this information as an up/down reading in feet per minute.

The pressure instruments – ASI, altimeter and VSI – all suffer from a slight lag in displaying information when airspeed, altitude, or rate of climb or descent change. Inexperienced student pilots often find themselves impatiently 'chasing' these instruments, making constant corrections instead of waiting for the instrument indications to stabilize and then taking action if necessary.

The artificial horizon operates on the gyroscopic principle. It provides information about the aircraft's attitude relative to the horizon. The instrument's face comprises an aircraft symbol combined with a horizon bar, which moves to show the aircraft's relative position: climbing, diving, banking left or right, or any combination of those conditions. This instrument provides vital information for flight when no outside visual references are available (in cloud for example).

The turn-and-slip indicator is also commonly known as the turn-and-bank indicator or turn co-ordinator. It is a two-part instrument, comprising a needle or, in more modern turn co-ordinators, a miniature aircraft that deflects left or right as appropriate when the aircraft banks into a turn. The other part of the display is a free-floating ball inside a spirit level. The ball remains centred when the aircraft is in a balanced or co-ordinated turn, but moves sideways if the aircraft is slipping (sliding sideways into the direction of the turn) or skidding (sliding outward, away from the direction of turn).

Engine and System Instruments

In a small training aircraft such as the Cessna 152, there are only a few engine and system instruments, and they are quite straightforward. Usually, they comprise a tachometer or rev-counter, which indicates engine revolutions per minute; oil temperature and oil pressure gauges for monitoring the engine's lubrication system; an alternator gauge that measures electrical load (like an ammeter in a car); and a suction gauge that monitors suction for the vacuum-driven gyroscopic instruments. Fuel-quantity gauges are also fitted to show how much fuel remains in the aircraft's tanks but, as a prudent pilot, you will always make a visual check of each tank's contents before flying, and monitor fuel consumption during each flight.

Navigation Instruments

The most common navigation instrument is still the old-fashioned magnetic compass. Usually, this takes the form of a bubble-type instrument mounted high up on top of the instrument panel glareshield or in the upper part of the windscreen. Magnetic compasses are slow in responding to an aircraft's directional changes, and are subject to acceleration errors and regional magnetic influences. For these reasons, a direction indicator or directional gyro is used for more precise navigation. However, the DI must be synchronized with the aircraft's magnetic compass before take-off and at regular intervals throughout a flight.

Later, during more advanced training, students will encounter two further navigation instruments: the automatic direction finder (ADF) and the VHF omni-directional range (VOR) receiver. The ADF is a radio compass with an indicator needle that points to the position of the ground station transmitter to which it is tuned. The VOR receives signals from ground stations that transmit those signals along each of the 360 degrees of the compass, or 'radials' as they are known. By tuning to a ground station within range and selecting a desired radial, a pilot can fly directly to, or away from, the station by keeping an indicator needle centred in the instrument display.

RADIO COMMUNICATIONS

All modern training aircraft have a very high frequency (VHF) transceiver for communicating with airfield control towers and other air traffic control ground facilities. Although some basic aircraft are equipped with cabin speakers for listening and hand-held microphones for speaking, most now employ individual headsets with boom microphones for the occupants. For training purposes, headsets are preferable because they permit the pupil and instructor to communicate easily through an intercom facility. Headsets offer the additional advantage of effectively excluding some engine and airflow noise, which unfortunately is an all-too-noticeable feature of light aircraft. When wearing a headset, the pilot transmits to ground stations by pressing a 'push-to-talk' (PTT) switch conveniently set into the hand-grip of each control wheel or stick.

Does it still sound daunting? Probably, if you are entirely unfamiliar with aircraft. However, rest assured that it will all seem much clearer when you see the aircraft's controls and instruments actually working. If you are still game to try, and you should be, read on.

Chapter 2
The Private Pilot
Licence

In the UK, there are two categories of licence available to the private pilot: the Private Pilot Licence (PPL) and the National Private Pilot Licence (NPPL). Although the NPPL (described in greater detail in Chapter 3) is the easier and cheaper to obtain, the PPL offers the advantage of fewer restrictions on the holder, and also is the first step on the ladder to a civilian aviation career. It is broadly equivalent to a full driving licence, permitting the holder to fly private aircraft for personal business and pleasure, and to carry passengers, provided no payment is received. A PPL (Aeroplanes) or PPL (Helicopters), therefore, is the starting point for nearly all non-commercial civilian, and all commercial, flying.

The more basic NPPL is a 'recreational' licence for those who intend to restrict their flying to the daytime in the UK only and to simple aircraft (including microlights). It has a shorter training syllabus and simpler medical requirements. Although an NPPL can be converted to a PPL at a later date if the holder wants to expand his or her flying activities, it would seem sensible to opt for the more 'senior' private licence at the beginning if there is a chance that this will happen. Other air sports, such as gliding, hang gliding and paragliding, have their own systems of pilot qualification and are outside the scope of this book.

No general academic qualifications are required to qualify for the issue of a licence, and there is no lower age limit at which you may start learning to fly. However, any flight time gained before the age of fourteen cannot be counted toward the experience requirements of the PPL. To apply to be cleared to fly solo while training, you must be at least sixteen, and you must be seventeen before a licence can be issued. At the other end of the scale, there is no upper age limit. Many people in their sixties and seventies have successfully completed PPL training courses.

Unlike the driving licence, which can be obtained by taking any haphazard form of tuition that will get an applicant through the test, a PPL is granted only after completion of a recognized syllabus of ground and flight instruction conducted by properly qualified flying instructors, and after successful passes have been obtained in ground examinations and flying tests. Although a pilot friend or relative can probably give you some basic

The two-seat Cessna 150 was introduced in the USA in the late 1950s and soon became established as a trainer around the world. In 1977, it was supplanted by the more powerful 152 model. This particular example is a 150 Aerobat, a specially strengthened version capable of performing basic aerobatics. (Adrian Pingstone)

experience at the controls of an aircraft, such experience cannot be counted toward the minimum number of hours required for the PPL course, unless he or she is a qualified flying instructor.

The licensing of pilots in the United Kingdom is the responsibility of the Civil Aviation Authority (CAA), whose records show that there are approximately 26,000 active PPL holders in the country, with over 3,000 new licences being issued annually. Until recently, the CAA operated under the rules of the European Community's Joint Aviation Authority (JAA), whose member states agreed to harmonize all matters relating to aviation under the umbrella of the Joint Aviation Requirements (JAR). This included flight crew licensing (FCL). Subsequently, however, responsibility for flight crew licensing throughout the member states of the EC was passed to the European Aviation Safety Agency (EASA).

The JAR-FCL syllabus for the PPL calls for a minimum of 45 hours of flying instruction. However, five of those training hours may be acquired in a synthetic flight trainer, which is a type of ground-based electronic flight simulator. The 45-hour figure is simply a statutory minimum requirement and does not guarantee that a licence will be granted automatically upon completion of that number of hours. In practice, the average qualifying time for students is between 55 and 60 hours of instruction, a fact to keep in mind when calculating the likely cost of obtaining your licence.

WHAT TO DO? WHERE TO GO?

There are more than 200 flying schools, clubs and training organizations in the United Kingdom. They vary in size from chummy one-man, one-aircraft businesses to large operations with fleets of a dozen or more aircraft, staffs of full-time instructors on call seven days a week and comprehensive facilities on the ground for classroom study.

What you are taught should not vary, because the training syllabuses, examinations and tests are standardized. How you are taught, the rate at which you progress, how much you pay and whether you get good value for your money will depend on wise selection of your training establishment, and probably on a bit of luck too. Big does not necessarily mean best, nor small, cheapest. A one-man outfit might provide a very personal touch, but consider what may happen to the continuity of your training if that one man goes sick, or his one aircraft is grounded for a prolonged period of maintenance.

How to Choose a Club or School

A selection of clubs and flight schools is given Chapter 6. The CAA maintains an up-to-date list of licensed training establishments on its web site. In fact, the internet is extremely useful in searching out flying clubs and schools, many of which have their own web sites. Simply enter something like 'flight training Sussex' in a search engine and you will be given a number of choices. From time to time, aviation magazines may print 'where-to-fly' guides; they also carry advertisements from some flying clubs and schools. Even your local *Yellow Pages* may offer some suggestions.

As a first step, obtain one of these lists and search out the operators in your area. How far you cast your net is up to you. However, do not assume that the school nearest you must be the one to choose. An airfield and a flying club within a mile or two of your home might appear ideal at first consideration, but there may be reasons why they are not the best choice. Much of your training will involve general flying in clear airspace, and if your local airfield is a commercial airport with its own protected airspace, you will have to spend time at the beginning and end of each lesson flying to and from a practice area. This could be good experience, but it will cost you money in flying time, during which you will not be progressing through the exercises of the PPL syllabus. At a busy airport, you may also find yourself frequently waiting in a line of aircraft all wanting to take off. Since charges for flying lessons are often costed from engine start to engine stop, or 'brakes off' to 'brakes on' in flying jargon, this can be a very expensive and unproductive traffic jam.

Airfields where many flying clubs and schools operate will also create traffic problems when it comes to the 'circuits and bumps' part of the PPL course, the part of the training when you spend many hours doing nothing but taking off, flying around the rectangular course of the airfield's traffic circuit, landing and taking off again. At a busy airfield, other aircraft may seriously restrict the number of circuits that can be flown in an hour's lesson. On the other hand, a busy airfield with a mix of commercial and private traffic will quickly breed confidence in radio and air-traffic procedures.

Having selected likely airfields within your reach, list the training establishments at each and pay them a visit. Do not be daunted if the airfield entrance is dotted with 'Keep Out' or 'Pilots Only' signs threatening dire peril to trespassers. They are only there to keep out inquisitive children. Invariably, weekends will be busy if the weather is reasonable, and therefore they are a good time to gain an impression of flying-school activity. That said, you may not receive the fullest attention from staff when they are busiest. A weekday visit would probably be better for asking questions, obtaining a tour of the facilities and looking over the aircraft.

Flying is very much an enthusiast's activity in Britain. An increasing number of flying clubs and schools, perhaps the majority, do have plush, sparkling premises with smartly dressed staff, airy classrooms and comfortable lounges. However, more than a few still operate from buildings left behind by the services after World War II, with facilities sometimes little improved in the meantime. Whether you select a small, homely club or a large flying training school is largely a matter of personal preference.

You can learn a great deal from your reception on your first visit. For a start, does anyone bother to ask if they can help you? Flying does generate legendary camaraderie among fellow pilots but, sad to say, strangers are not universally accorded a warm welcome, even from those very people whose business it is to win over new customers. If your reception is too offhand, go somewhere where they do want your business. Otherwise, explain that you think you might like to learn to fly and ask if someone can answer a few questions. Prepare your questions in advance, ideally written down, and note down the answers you receive. Pilots and instructors tend to talk in abbreviations and jargon, so do not be afraid to ask for an explanation of anything that appears to be expressed in a secret language.

You should ask how many training aircraft are operated by the club or school. This can be very important. If there are just two in the fleet, for instance, the chances of lessons being delayed or cancelled through technical faults, or because the last pilot did not return the aircraft on time, can be very high. Ask if the school has its own, or readily available, maintenance facilities to ensure aircraft reliability and availability. How many instructors are there, and what is the student/instructor ratio? Is there an efficient system for booking lessons that will ensure you get the instructor you want?

Flying instruction is not a well-paid profession at private-pilot level. As a result, the instructional staff at many clubs and schools is often made up of young aspiring professional pilots, and there can be a rapid turnover among instructors, which can lead to discontinuity in training. An occasional change of tutors can be refreshing, but having a different instructor for every lesson is a frustrating and expensive business, because you might find yourself going over some parts of the PPL course many times while never touching others.

It is unlikely that many schools could guarantee one-to-one instruction from the same instructor throughout a PPL course, but one that has a good number of older full-time professional flying instructors on staff should score highly on your list of possibilities.

Ask to see the ground training facilities. Are there proper classrooms, lecture rooms, or at least individual briefing cubicles for study, and for pre- and post-flight discussions with your instructor? Does the school run classes, in the evenings or at weekends, for the PPL examination subjects? Ground school is just as important as flying on the road to gaining a PPL. There is nothing worse than trying to master complex theory or solve a tricky navigational problem in a noisy office with a telephone ringing, or in a club bar surrounded by chattering pilots, beeping video-game machines and demented one-armed bandits.

Note also whether the whole operation is run in an efficient and businesslike manner. Are the premises and aircraft clean, and well cared for? It is reasonable to assume that a seedy looking and run-down operation may adopt a similarly careless attitude toward your training. You may get your licence eventually, but it will have cost more and taken longer than it should have done.

Try to talk with other students at the club or school. Ask what they think of it, and how they have progressed with their training. However, do not believe everything you hear. Every activity has its share of 'professional' moaners who can find fault with everyone and everything, but a high number of complaints should be taken as a warning that all may not be well.

Trial Lessons

Most flying schools offer trial lessons, and you should take advantage of this, at least at those schools that seem to meet all other requirements. Do not be alarmed at the term 'trial'. It is flying that is on trial, not you. The purpose of the flight is to acquaint you with the sensations of flight in a small aircraft and to demonstrate the basic effects of the aircraft's controls, not to decide whether you have the makings of a pilot.

A trial lesson, sometimes called an air-experience flight, usually lasts about 30 minutes. The cost will vary from one establishment to another, but often is around half the cost of a full hour's dual instruction, depending on the package. The schools with the lower costs usually carry out the flights on a subsidized basis, in the hope that the potential student will become hooked. Most provide a basic ground briefing followed by about 30 minutes in the air, during which time you should be given the opportunity to handle the aircraft yourself.

There are companies that offer vouchers that allow you to get a taste of a variety of sporting activities, including flying. In the latter case, these are redeemable at a number of flying schools around the country. However, they may not always offer the best value, particularly when compared with going directly to a school. Check a few prices first before choosing this option.

No matter how you go about booking your trial flight, a considerate school will arrange your first light aircraft trip on a calm day with good visibility, free from gusting winds, turbulence or low clouds, which are not good introductions to flying. The lesson should begin with a pre-flight briefing on what you are going to do in the air, followed by a practical introduction to aviating with you handling the controls under the instructor's supervision. If you get no more than a sightseeing ride with the instructor remaining steadfastly silent and not relinquishing the controls for a moment, suspect the worst of the school concerned.

Several facts will quickly emerge during your trial flight. Flying in a light aircraft is not at all like riding in the claustrophobic confines of a large airliner. You will fly much lower and enjoy a fine panoramic view of the world below, which is denied to those who can only peer through the few square inches of an airliner's window. You will also discover, however, that the cockpit of a two-seat training aircraft is noisy and often cramped, which makes it a poor classroom in which to absorb theory and further emphasizes the need for proper ground study facilities at the school, where your instructor can brief you in peace and quiet. The use of headsets with an intercom will overcome some of the problems of effective instructor/student communication, and reduce the fatiguing effects of engine noise.

Still Keen to Become a Pilot?

If the trial lesson has whetted your appetite for flying, now is the time to talk to your selected school about booking a course of lessons for the PPL syllabus. Because the number of hours needed to qualify for a PPL will vary from one individual to another, depending on how quickly they master the necessary skills, most schools provide flying tuition by the hour, rather than signing up students for a complete course from the outset. Some do offer fixed-price courses, however, so check first to see if it is a guaranteed 'get-your-licence' deal. It may be that the course fee includes only the statutory minimum of 45 hours of flying, which almost certainly will not be enough. Otherwise, you pay as you go, usually at an hourly rate, or pro rata against the time from an engine start to engine stop. Dual flying – flight time with an instructor – usually comes a little more expensive than solo use of an aircraft, typically by a few pounds more per hour, although many schools now adopt a higher 'training' charge rate throughout a course, irrespective of whether the student is accompanied by an instructor or flying solo.

How Much Will it Cost?

Hourly charges vary from school to school, for different aircraft, and in different geographical locations. In 2008, a typical hourly charge for dual instruction in a Cessna 152 or Piper Tomahawk class of aircraft, including VAT, was about £110, but it can be considerably higher, in the London area for example. On the assumption that it will take some 55 hours to complete the course, a sum of about £6,000 should therefore be regarded as the likely

For the qualified private pilot looking for a step up from the basic trainer, Cessna's 172 Skyhawk provides four seats in a familiar-looking airframe. Like its smaller brother, the Cessna 150/152, the 172 has been around for decades in many different models. The latest example, the Skyhawk SP, has a fuel-injected engine delivering 180hp. (Cessna Aircraft Company)

cost of the flying element of a PPL course. Add the medical examination fee, the cost of books, maps and ancillary equipment, examination and flight test charges, and the licence issue fee, and around £6,500 is a realistic assessment of the total outlay required. You will find PPL courses offered for much less but, whatever rate you are quoted, do make sure that you determine exactly what the charge includes. Schools have been known to attract business by offering seemingly generous hourly rates while neglecting to point out that they do not include such non-optional extras as pre-flight briefings, instructor's time, airport landing fees and VAT.

Some schools will arrange personal loans through finance companies to pay for flying tuition. Practically all of them also accept popular credit cards for payment, and it is not totally unknown for understanding bank managers to offer loans. It is worth asking a school if it gives a discount for block bookings, such as 10 hours of instruction paid for in advance. This can provide a useful saving. In general, however, parting with too large a sum in advance is not wise. It is possible that you may decide to give up before completing the course or, as has happened to a number of unfortunate students, the school could go out of business. Payments by credit card can protect you from suffering a loss, as if the school does cease trading, the credit card company will reimburse you, within certain conditions. From the school's point of view, however, it will be unable to offer much of a discount if it has to pay a significant percentage of its profit to the card company.

Almost certainly, you will be asked to become a member of the school or club. This is a normal insurance prerequisite for flying its aircraft. You will be asked to pay a one-time joining fee and an annual subscription thereafter, which entitles you to use all of the club's facilities and join in social activities.

Most clubs also offer family or social membership for spouses, children and friends, which enables them to fly as passengers in club aircraft. Apart from flying, you will find that most clubs and schools arrange social activities, and many have a bar, but strictly for after-flying drinking!

Regarding insurance, do check that the club or school holds appropriate aircraft and liability cover that indemnifies you against claims if you are unfortunate enough to have an accident or incident while flying. Do not be afraid to ask to see the current policy and aircraft certificates. Nowadays, the policy wordings are in 'plain English', so it should be relatively easy to check that all pilots flying club aircraft are covered for public and passenger liability. A reputable school will be happy to provide evidence of such cover. This is very important. Even a minor accident on the ground can cause very expensive damage to an aircraft. A crash involving other people, aircraft or property could result in potentially ruinous claims. If you have a personal accident policy or intend taking out a life assurance policy after you have taken up flying training, be sure to tell the company that you are learning to fly. Otherwise, the policy will contain a clause that excludes cover while the policy-holder is in an aircraft, except as a fare-paying passenger, or words to that effect. Cover for private flying can usually be obtained for a very small increase in premium. If your insurance company tries to tell you otherwise, look for another one. Life policies taken out before you intended taking up flying are unaffected.

Are You Fit Enough to be a Pilot?

Although you do not have to meet any medical standards before starting to learn to fly, before you can fly a powered aircraft solo, and consequently before you can obtain your PPL, you must have a valid medical certificate. It is strongly recommended that you obtain a medical certificate before you commit to a full PPL course. This will avoid the possible frustration of going through the expense and training up to the level of your first solo, and then discovering that you are unable to pass the medical. Note that the medical requirements for an NPPL are less stringent than those for a PPL; they are discussed in Chapter 3.

Contrary to popular myth, you do not have to be super-fit astronaut material to become a pilot. Although airline and military pilots are required to maintain very high levels of physical fitness, which are constantly monitored, the JAR Class 2 medical certificate currently needed for a PPL sets much less demanding standards. Note that if you intend to go on to train for a professional licence, it is more sensible to obtain the more demanding JAR Class 1 medical certificate necessary for such a licence from the outset.

To obtain a medical certificate, you must undergo an examination by a doctor authorized by the CAA to carry out such tests. Your local general practitioner cannot conduct the examination unless he or she is a CAA Authorized Medical Examiner (AME), or you are seeking to gain an NPPL or other 'recreational' type of licence. However, there is a good geographic spread of AMEs throughout the country. Most large towns have one, and your flying school can probably give you a list of those practising in the local area. Alternatively, check out the CAA's web site. Some larger airports have facilities for a medical to be carried out 'in house', with an AME making regular visits to the airport surgery. Appointments may usually be booked through the main flying club based at the airfield.

The straightforward medical examination has to be paid for at the time, and fees vary according to the doctor and scope of examination required. Before attending the examination, you must obtain an application form (CAA Medical Form 160), which will be available from your AME, or you can download it from the CAA's web site. The form includes a personal health questionnaire detailing significant medical conditions from which you may have suffered – you may need to obtain information concerning such conditions from your general practitioner and present it at the examination. Although the relevance of some questions may not be apparent, the form should be completed as fully and truthfully as you are able. The doctor will check eyesight, hearing, reflexes, respiratory system and blood pressure, among other things. A resting electrocardiogram (ECG) is required prior to the issue of your first medical certificate, which may necessitate a hospital visit. Alternatively, the results of the ECG may need to be interpreted by a local cardiologist, which may delay the issue of the certificate. Subsequently, for those aged over forty, an ECG will be required each time the certificate is renewed.

If all is well, your medical certificate will be issued. This may take place at the time of the examination if the AME is qualified to interpret the results of the ECG.

All licensed pilots must hold a current medical certificate for their licence to remain valid, and must inform the CAA in writing of any injury or medical condition that might invalidate the certificate.

Anyone in good health and of average fitness should have no problem in passing the JAR Class 2 medical examination. Certain complaints, such as epilepsy, diabetes requiring medication for control and cardiac problems normally preclude the granting of a medical certificate. For this reason, and because some disqualifying conditions may not be known to the would-be pilot, applying for a medical certificate before starting training is essential. Eyesight defects that are correctable with spectacles or contact lenses are usually acceptable – you should take your latest prescription with you to the examination. If the vision is outside specific parameters without glasses, the medical certificate will probably be endorsed with a requirement for the holder to carry a spare pair of spectacles when flying as a precaution against loss or breakage in the air.

The JAR Class 2 medical certificate is valid for five years for those aged under forty, two years for the under-fifties, and one year for those aged over fifty. However, any five-year certificate issued prior to the holder's fortieth birthday will cease to be valid after the age of forty-two.

The loss of limbs or other physical impairment does not automatically exclude one from becoming a private pilot. Many paraplegics have successfully gained their licences, and there is an annual sponsorship scheme detailed in this book that provides PPL training for the disabled. The CAA requirement is that a disabled pilot must be able to operate all of the aircraft's controls fully. Adapted aircraft controls, such as those that enable the rudder to be operated by hand instead of by the feet, may be acceptable, provided that control movement is not restricted. Quick-conversion kits to modify aircraft for disabled pilots have been developed for many common training types. The CAA Medical Branch examines each disabled applicant for a PPL medical certificate on merit. Far from being ogres, the staff are most anxious to assist anyone with medical problems to get into the air if it is possible within the constraints of safety.

THE PPL COURSE

We have already noted that the course for the JAR-FCL PPL is of a minimum 45 hours duration, 5 hours of which can be completed in a ground-based flight trainer or simulator. It must be conducted to a syllabus recognized by the CAA, and comprises an integrated programme of flying and ground

Private Pilot Licence – Aeroplanes: Requirements		
PPL(A) 45hr of flight time minimum	Up to 5hr may be on a flight navigation procedural trainer or flight simulator approved by the CAA	
	10% of total flight time as pilot-in-command, up to a maximum of 10hr, may be credited toward the 45hr by holders of pilot licences for helicopters, microlights (having fixed wings and movable aerodynamic control surfaces acting in all three dimensions), gliders, or self-sustaining gliders or self-launching gliders	
	25hr dual instruction	
	10hr supervised solo flight time	5hr solo cross-country flight time, including a flight of at least 150 nautical miles that visits and lands at two aerodromes
	The balance of hours, if not claimed on a simulator or trainer, or by existing licence holders, must be made up of supervised solo flight time or dual instruction	

tuition. The school or club is required to keep detailed records of each student's progress to ensure that training has been carried out systematically.

Details of the PPL syllabus are contained in the CAA publication *LASORS*, which provides a variety of valuable information on licensing requirements and aviation safety.

The JAR-FCL PPL flight training syllabus is divided into a sequence of numbered exercises:

1. Familiarization with the aircraft.
2. Preparation for and action after flight.
3. Air experience.
4. Effects of controls.
5. Taxiing.
6. Straight and level flight.
7. Climbing.
8. Descending.
9. Turning.
10. Slow flight.
11. Spin avoidance.
12. Take-off and climb to downwind position.
13. Circuit, approach and landing.
14. First solo.
15. Advanced turning.
16. Forced landing without power.
17. Precautionary landing.
18. Navigation.
19. Basic instrument flight.

Exercise 1 provides an introduction to the aircraft and its systems. It also covers the actions necessary in the event of an emergency, such as fire on the ground or in the air, together with escape drills and use of emergency equipment.

Exercise 2 covers the actions before and after a flight, such as the necessary paperwork, the equipment required, checking the aircraft, starting and warming the engine, and shutting it down.

Exercise 3 is a general introduction to flying the aircraft, giving you experience in the air.

Exercise 4 will demonstrate the purpose of the various controls and show how their movement affects the aircraft. It will also indicate how controls can have secondary affects on the aircraft.

Exercise 5 provides experience of manoeuvring the aircraft on the ground, including controlling speed, turning, stopping and parking. Emergencies, such as brake or steering failure, will also be covered.

Exercise 6 will teach you how to fly the aircraft straight and level, which is a vital skill. You will be shown how to control the aircraft at normal cruising speed and at high speeds, how to use the trimmer and how to maintain direction, using the instruments for precision.

Exercise 7 covers climbing the aircraft, including entering the climb, maintaining the climb at normal and maximum rates, how to level off at a specified altitude and how to use the instruments for precision.

Exercise 8 covers descending the aircraft, including entering the descent, maintaining the descent and levelling off at specified altitudes. Descent with and without power will also be covered, as will the use of instruments and side-slipping.

Exercise 9 will teach you how to make balanced turns at a required rate while in level flight, climbing and descending. Also, you will learn how to stop a turn on a required heading, using the aircraft's magnetic compass and gyro heading indicator.

Exercise 10 is split into two parts: A and B. Exercise 10A concerns slow flight and teaches the student how to recognize when the aircraft has slowed inadvertently to a dangerous speed and what to do to regain normal cruising or climb speed. Exercise 10B covers stalling (when the aircraft slows sufficiently that the wings no longer provide lift). This exercise teaches you to recognize the stalled condition and what to do to recover from the situation. Stall recovery will be practised with and without power.

Exercise 11 will show you how to recognize and prevent an extension of the stalled condition, the spin (caused by excessive wing drop during the stall).

Exercise 12 will teach you how to take off and climb to the downwind position in the airfield's traffic circuit. You will be shown the required pre-take-off checks, how to take off into wind and with a crosswind, how to make a short-field take-off and how to implement noise-abatement procedures. You will also be taught how to deal with an emergency, such as abandoning a take-off and coping with an engine failure after take-off.

Exercise 13 continues the circuit from the downwind position to the approach and landing. You will be taught the required circuit procedures, how to make glide and powered approaches, how to make an approach with and without flaps, how to deal with a crosswind, how to make a short-field landing, and how to carry out a missed-approach and go-around.

Exercise 14 This is the big one, the first solo flight, that unrepeatable moment, the high point of every pilot's life, from novice to airline captain, when first you are in sole command of an aircraft. When will you go solo? When your instructor thinks you are ready, and not before. You must hold a medical certificate before you go solo, and most flying clubs will insist that you pass the air law examination, which is a sensible safety requirement. Most students are sent off on their first solo circuit of the airfield when they have completed between 10 and 12 hours of dual instruction. There is no set time in the syllabus, however, and the figure will vary from one individual to another, depending on their aptitude. Contrary to popular belief, going solo does not mean that you have gained your wings and become a pilot. Far from it. It is a confidence-building exercise, which assures you that your instructor has faith that you can take off, fly around the airfield circuit pattern, land and cope with any likely emergencies that might occur. Nothing more. Just when that golden moment comes and you write 'first solo' in your pilot's log book (usually in unnecessarily large and shaky handwriting) depends mostly on your own ability and rate of learning, so take no notice of 'experts' who tell you that unless you go solo in 'x' number of hours, you stand no chance of gaining your licence. You may be sure that if you go on for too long before showing signs of reaching solo standard, your instructor will tell you.

Exercise 15 gives you experience in making steep turns (45 degrees) in level and descending flight, plus the techniques required to recover from a stall during a steep turn. You will also be taught how to recover from unusual attitudes, including a spiral dive.

Exercise 16 looks at forced-landing techniques, teaching you how to select a suitable landing area, how to prepare a descent plan, how to carry out engine failure checks and make the necessary emergency radio calls, and how to carry out the final approach and landing. Checks to be made after landing will also be covered.

Exercise 17 will show you how to carry out a precautionary landing away from the airfield. You will be taught the conditions that might make this necessary, how to select a suitable area, how to plan the circuit and approach and what to do after landing.

Exercise 18 is split into three sections: A, B and C. Exercise 18A covers basic navigation, including flight planning, compass turns and map reading, maintaining heading, log keeping, use of the radio and navigation aids, carrying out a diversion to an alternative airfield, what to do if you become uncertain of your position, and procedures upon arrival at your destination. Exercise 18B concerns navigation at low level and in reduced visibility. It covers hazards, the difficulties of map reading, the effects of wind and turbulence, avoidance of noise-sensitive areas, and how to carry out a bad weather circuit and landing. In Exercise 18C, radio navigation and radar services are covered, the student being shown how to use a variety of systems, including VHF omni-directional range (VOR), automatic direction finding (ADF) equipment, VHF direction finding (VHF/DF) equipment, distance measuring equipment (DME) and en-route/terminal radar, including transponders.

Exercise 19 is the final exercise. It teaches instrument appreciation, but only to a level of safe flight on instruments, not navigation.

In most cases, you are unlikely to spend an entire lesson on one exercise; instead, aspects of several will be combined, and you will probably go over these again in subsequent lessons. Throughout your training, your instructor will stress the importance of good airmanship. During your training, you will be required to complete at least 5 hours of solo cross-country flying, which must include one flight of at least 150 nautical miles, during which landings at two separate airfields (different to your departure airfield) must be made.

Controllers at the airfields visited will sign a landing card to confirm your visit, being invited to observe and comment on your circuit discipline and landing procedure.

Once you have completed the course, you must take the Skill Test within six months. A successful pass of the test is valid for twelve months.

How long will the PPL course take?

Again, this depends on many factors, perhaps most important of which is the frequency of the lessons. Continuity is vitally important in any learning process, in none more so than in flying, and in the early stages it will certainly determine how quickly you go solo. Invariably, long gaps between lessons will mean spending a period of each detail re-learning something forgotten from the previous session. Inevitably, this will increase the duration and cost of the entire course.

If possible, try to fly at least once a week, preferably more frequently. Best of all, if you can set aside a period of two or three weeks, flying each day as weather permits, you can probably cover a substantial portion of the syllabus quite quickly. Bear in mind, though, that flying instruction and all light aircraft operation is very dependent upon the weather. The UK student who claims not to have had a few lessons cancelled because of unsuitable conditions either has a bad memory or is incredibly lucky. It is frustrating, but you will have to learn to live with it. Aircraft also have a habit of developing niggling faults just as you are about to fly. Therefore, it is inadvisable to try to fit a flying lesson into a day on which you have a busy programme of work or social commitments. Rather, set aside an entire day and schedule more than one lesson, with time between each for ground study of the exercises to be flown. You can help keep the school's schedule running smoothly by always arriving in plenty of time for pre-flight briefings from your instructor and for checking the aircraft before flying. If you have to cancel a lesson for any reason, do try to give the school as much advance notice as possible, so that the aircraft and instructor can be allocated to another student if required. Next time, it could be you waiting to fit in another hour of flying.

Some flying schools offer full-time residential courses for the PPL, which aim to complete the course within a few weeks. This is an excellent idea, provided you can spare the time and money, with the caveat that the British weather is an unwelcome and often unco-operative intruder into the best-organized courses.

Ground School

The ground training element of the JAR-FCL PPL syllabus covers the following technical subjects:

• Air Law and Operational Procedures.
• Human Performance and Limitations.

- Navigation and Radio Aids.
- Meteorology.
- Aircraft (General) and Principles of Flight.
- Flight Performance and Planning.
- Communications.

Ground training, or ground school, is an important and statutory part of the PPL syllabus. It must be closely co-ordinated with flying training so that the relevant subjects and procedures have been studied on the ground before they are put into practice in the air. A considerable amount of study will be needed to prepare for the PPL examinations, which must be passed before a licence is issued. Again, it is difficult to put a precise figure on the time needed, as it varies from one student to another, depending on their ability to learn, but 50–100 hours is accepted as an average figure.

Although pre- and post-flight briefings from your instructor should be essential parts of each flying lesson, few flying schools offer one-to-one teaching for the ground examinations, unless you are prepared to pay for an instructor's time to give you individual tuition. Most offer lecture courses for groups of student pilots, often conducted as evening classes, for which a separate, usually modest, charge is made. Audio-visual courses using video and aural tapes are also employed. Some further-education centres may also offer tuition, and a few schools run week-long or weekend courses covering the entire PPL ground-school syllabus, including sitting the technical examinations, with on-site accommodation if required. Home-study courses are also available, often including inter-active CD-ROMs that cover all of the PPL subjects. These allow you to put your home computer to good use.

Your progress through the PPL course will be monitored by the school. The CAA recommends that schools issue students with copies of their syllabus, which they can sign upon completion of each phase of training, agreeing that the items have been covered. You will also keep a record of your flying hours in your Personal Flying Log Book, which every student must submit with the licence application at the end of the course. Your log book is an important document – the only official record of your flying time – and it must be maintained throughout your flying life.

The Tests

Before you can apply for a PPL, you must pass written and oral examinations, and take practical tests. The examinations consist of written papers on the seven technical subjects listed previously, together with an oral technical quiz on the specific aircraft type on which you have trained. The written examination questions are of the multiple-choice type: for example, *Flaps are fitted to aircraft to: a) Increase lift and drag while lowering stalling speed; b) Increase drag, payload and stalling angle; or c) Increase lift, drag and stalling speed*. The correct answer is *(a)*.

The technical examinations and oral test are usually taken at your flying school, and different amounts of time are allowed for the various papers, which vary in number of questions as follows:

- Air Law and Operational Procedures – 40 questions, 60 minutes.
- Human Performance and Limitations – 20 questions, 30 minutes.
- Navigation and Radio Aids – 25 questions, 90 minutes.
- Meteorology – 20 questions, 60 minutes.
- Aircraft (General) and Principles of Flight – 50 questions, 90 minutes.
- Flight Performance and Planning – 20 questions, 60 minutes.
- Communications – 30 questions, 40 minutes.

The pass mark for each examination is seventy-five per cent. You do not have to sit all the examinations at once; you simply take each of them when you feel you are sufficiently knowledgeable, and you do not have to take them in any particular order, although it is wise to have passed particular examinations before certain critical points in your training, as explained later. Those that you fail have to be sat again, but there is a statutory two-week delay before you can take an exam for the second time. If you fail again, you have to wait four weeks before making a third attempt. A third failure will require that you receive further training by your school before sitting the examination for the fourth time at a CAA centre. This time, if you fail, you will have to wait three months and then take *all* the examinations again, but at a CAA centre and after further training.

It is recommended that Air Law and Operational Procedures, Human Performance and Limitations, and Communications be passed before making the first solo flight, while Navigation, Meteorology, and Flight Performance and Planning will be helpful when you come to the Navigation exercises of the course. Prior to the first solo cross-country flight, it is sensible to have taken the practical radiotelephony test (*see* later). All the theoretical tests must be passed before taking the final PPL Skill Test, and must be completed within an eighteen-month period. The pass results will be accepted toward the grant of a PPL during the twenty-four months from the date of successfully completing the examinations.

The Skill Test is the final hurdle before the issue of your licence. Including pre- and post-flight briefings, it may last as long as 4½ hours. The flight itself comprises five sections:

1. Departure.
2. Airwork.
3. En-route Procedures.
4. Approach and Landing.
5. Abnormal and Emergency Procedures.

It is intended to be flown as a complete flight, including navigation and general handling procedures, although by agreement between applicant and

The Piper PA-32 Cherokee Six can carry six people and clearly is derived from the smaller PA-28. Some later versions had retractable landing gear. Such aircraft are among many available to the private pilot. (Adrian Pingstone)

examiner, Section 3, which includes navigation, may be flown as a separate flight of a minimum duration of one hour.

The Skill Test, as its name implies, examines the student's competence in the exercises of the PPL flying syllabus, any (or all) of which you may be asked to demonstrate to the examiner's satisfaction during the flight. During the en-route phase, the examiner assesses the student pilot's flight planning; handling of air traffic control instructions; dead-reckoning navigation, map reading; ability to maintain course, altitude and airspeed at normal and low levels; ability to establish position visually after disruption of the planned flight; and to carry out a practice diversion to an alternative destination in simulated poor weather conditions. The use of navigation aids must be demonstrated and radar headings, provided they do not cause the aircraft to enter cloud. In addition, at some point in the flight, the examiner will ask the student pilot to carry out a 180-degree turn on instruments to demonstrate the ability to recover from an inadvertent entry into cloud.

If you fail one of the sections, the examiner will advise you of those aspects of your flying that need refining, and after some further dual instruction and practice, you can take that section again (together with Section 1). If you fail two or more sections, however, you will have to take the entire Skill Test again, usually after an additional period of training. There is no limit to the number of Skill Tests you may take.

Most large flying schools have a CAA-delegated examiner on staff, so unlike the driving test, you do not have to apply months in advance to take your PPL Skill Test.

Radio Communications
For student pilots, learning to fly also means mastering the use of the aircraft's VHF radio transmitter for two-way communication with airport

35

control towers and other air traffic control facilities on the ground. Radiotelephony (RT) training is an integral part of the PPL syllabus, and leads to a test for the issue of a Flight Radiotelephony Operator Licence, popularly known as the RT Licence, which is a separate document to the JAR-FCL PPL.

Therefore, a student pilot must learn the language of aviation. Not the 'Bandits at five o'clock, angels one-five, over and out' banter of the movies, but the precise language of air traffic control, which has two functions: to convey the maximum information in the fewest words, and to avoid ambiguity, which could lead to a misunderstanding and result in an accident.

'Affirm' is substituted for 'Yes', 'Negative' for 'No', and the phonetic alphabet, A-alpha, B-bravo and so on, is used when anything needs spelling out or abbreviating to initials. Once you overcome microphone nerves and learn to relax, you should slip into the correct phraseology without stumbling over your words. Books and interactive CD-ROMs are available to teach RT technique. You might also find an airband VHF radio useful for tuning in to airport and ATC frequencies to get the feel of radio procedures. A written examination and practical RT test, again usually conducted by your flying school, must be passed before an RT licence is issued. However, it is more usual for an instructor's certification of practical in-flight RT training and assessment of competence to be accepted in lieu of the practical test, avoiding the need for the separate tests.

The Licence

Once you have completed your PPL course, technical examinations and Skill Test, your examiner will send your examination results, Personal Flying Log Book and PPL application form to the CAA, which will enter a Certificate of Test in your log book and return it with your brand-new PPL.

Many non-fliers suppose that a PPL gives you the right to fly any aircraft. Sensibly, this is not so. The aircraft that licence holders are privileged to fly are set out in Aircraft Ratings included in the licence. These ratings are sub-qualifications that specify in detail the privileges that the licence provides. Where aircraft are concerned, they may be Class Ratings or Type Ratings. The former permits a broad class of machines to be flown, while the latter refers to a specific type or group of closely related aircraft. Other ratings are available that permit the holder to fly on instruments and at night. These will be explained more fully later.

The aircraft flown during the Skill Test for the PPL will allow you to obtain your first Aircraft Rating. With few exceptions, this will be a Single Engine Piston Landplane (SEP) Class Rating, which allows you to fly simple land-based aircraft with a non-turbocharged, single-piston engine, a fixed-pitch propellor, a fixed tricycle landing gear, an unpressurized cabin and a weight of less than 5,700kg. In theory, that allows a broad range of aircraft types that you could fly quite legally. In practice, however, if you are hiring aircraft from the club or school where you learned to fly, you are likely to be restricted to the aircraft type on which you trained, or something very similar in terms of performance, complexity and handling, until you have gained more experience. Insurance premiums, or the availability of cover, are also likely to impose similar constraints even if you buy your own aircraft.

Subsequently, you can extend the range of aircraft you can fly by taking differences training. There are five categories of difference:

- Tailwheel aircraft.
- Retractable landing gear.
- Variable-pitch propellor.
- Turbocharged engine.
- Cabin pressurization.

You do not have to take a test after differences training; your instructor simply signs off the training in your log book.

Other Class Ratings can also be added, after a suitable period of training and a Skill Test. These include:

- Multi-Engine Piston (MEP) landplane.
- Single- and Multi-Engined Piston seaplane.
- Touring Motor Glider (TMG).

Type Ratings usually relate to aircraft weighing more than 5,700kg, turbine aircraft and particularly complex machines. Again, a period of training is required, followed by a Skill Test.

There are other restrictions to the basic PPL. You may not fly in airways-designated airspace, which effectively forms the 'motorways' of the air-traffic system. You must remain in sight of the earth's surface, not in or above cloud, and with a minimum in-flight visibility of between 3 and 10km, dependent upon various criteria. The detailed privileges and exemptions applying to the PPL are many and cannot be listed in depth here. The CAA publication *LASORS* gives further information and should be consulted for specific details.

Although the licence is yours for life, it is valid for a period of five years, and must be revalidated at the end of that time. In addition, you must maintain the validity of the Class and Type Ratings to be able to continue flying the aircraft to which they apply. The Aircraft Ratings have different revalidation requirements, depending on the type and complexity of the machine. In the case of the basic SEP Class Rating, this is valid for a period of twenty-four months and must be revalidated within the three months preceding expiry. Revalidation requires that you have flown at least twelve hours in the previous twelve months in the relevant aircraft, that at least six of those hours were as sole pilot-in-command (PIC), that at least one hour was with an authorized instructor (who will endorse your log book), and that you made twelve take-offs and twelve landings during the period. If you cannot meet that experience, you must take a Licence Proficiency Check with an authorized examiner.

If you allow your licence or rating actually to expire, you will need to take a Licence Skills Test with an authorized examiner.

The validity of your PPL also depends on possession of a current medical certificate. If your certificate expires, or you fail a renewal examination, your PPL automatically becomes invalid until a medical certificate is reissued.

Can you carry passengers?

Certainly, provided they do not pay you an element of profit for your services as a pilot and you comply with the 'recency' rule (three take-offs and landings within the previous ninety days). The PPL is strictly an amateur licence in the literal sense, specifically forbidding flying for 'valuable consideration', although the acceptance of awards or prizes in amateur flying events, such as races or rallies, is permitted. Cost sharing between a pilot and no more than three passengers does fall within the privileges of the licence, however, provided all, including the pilot, pay an equal share. Personal business users can legitimately pay the full costs of a trip from a personal or partnership business account, and an employee can claim reimbursement from an employer without such payments being considered illegal.

You can fly abroad with a PPL; the licence is widely recognized (particularly in Europe). If you are flying a British-registered aircraft, there should be no problem in operating in foreign countries, provided you comply with all the necessary customs, immigration and air traffic procedures. If you want to hire a foreign-registered aircraft while in a country other than a JAA member state, you will need to validate your PPL for the country in question. This should be done in advance, since the time taken can vary from a few minutes spent form-filling to six months of negotiation, depending on the country with which you are dealing. You will probably have to take an examination in local air law and have a check ride with the operator hiring you the aircraft. In JAA member states, there should be few problems, as their aircraft will be JAA registered, allowing any JAR-FCL PPL holder to fly them without problems. Even if not required by law, a check ride or briefing of local customs will be well worth paying for.

Check rides are also necessary in Britain if you want to hire an aircraft from a club where you are not known. This may also be a requirement at your local club if you have not flown recently. Just how recently you must have flown will vary from club to club. Some insist on a check-out with an instructor, which you will be required to pay for, if you have not flown within a month, so there is a further spur to keep in regular flying practice.

HELICOPTERS

The foregoing summary of private pilot training is directed at those seeking to learn to fly fixed-wing light aircraft for the issue of a PPL (Aeroplanes).

However, learning to fly from scratch on helicopters is possible for the PPL (Helicopters). The JAR course duration is currently a minimum of 45 hours, as for fixed-wing aircraft, and the examinations and testing requirements are also identical, although certain aspects of the flying syllabus vary to incorporate those exercises specifically related to rotary-winged flight and to omit some manoeuvres. Stalling, for example, cannot be performed in a helicopter. The minimum course duration must include at least 25 hours of dual instruction and a minimum of 10 hours of supervised solo time. The latter must include at least 5 hours of solo cross-country time, during which one cross-country flight of at least 100 nautical miles must be made with landings at two separate airfields (excluding the departure airfield). The balance of hours is made up of other specified training. Five hours may be completed in a ground-based flight simulator. Upon completion of the course, and having passed all the relevant ground examinations, the student can take the Skill Test. This takes a similar form to the fixed-wing test, the student being required to demonstrate all the skills gained during training, including navigation. However, with the agreement of the examiner, the navigation portion of the test may be flown as a separate flight. A successful pass of the Skill Test will result in the issue of a JAR-FCL PPL(H).

Under current legislation, holders of licences for fixed-wing aircraft, three-axis microlights, microlight helicopters, gyroplanes, gliders or self-launching motor gliders are permitted to reduce the mimimum experience requirement on helicopters by ten per cent of their total time as pilot-in-command (PIC) on other machines (up to a maximum of 6 hours) if they are adding a PPL(H) to their qualifications. A similar reduction also applies to helicopter pilots seeking a fixed-wing PPL (again by ten per cent of their PIC time, up to a maximum of 10 hours).

The PPL(H) applicant must hold a valid JAR Class 1 or 2 medical certificate, although the former would only be necessary if the student intended to go on to obtain a commercial licence of some form. The ground-school examinations are similar to the PPL (A) exams, but with certain differences applicable to the operation of helicopters. The following subjects are covered:

- Air Law and Operational Procedures.
- Human Performance and Limitations.
- Navigation and Radio Aids.
- Meteorology.
- Aircraft (General) and Principles of Flight.
- Flight Performance and Planning.
- Communications.

Helicopter flying training schools are becoming increasingly common. The cost of helicopter operation is much greater than that of light aircraft, however, although the popularity of light piston-engined helicopters

Although still much more expensive than fixed-wing tuition, the cost of helicopter training has been kept down by the introduction of the popular two-seat Robinson R22, which is powered by an air-cooled, flat-four Lycoming engine. A larger four-seat model, the R44, is also available. (Robinson Helicopter Company)

(particularly the two-seat Robinson R22, which is widely used for rotary-wing training in the UK) has helped reduce the cost of obtaining a PPL(H). At 2008 rates, you could expect to pay around £275 per hour for instruction on a Robinson R22, and at least double that figure for flying a turbine-engine Bell JetRanger.

TRAINING ABROAD

Recent years have seen a tremendous increase in the number of companies offering overseas 'package' training courses. In the main, these are based in the USA, and to a lesser extent in France, where more dependable weather can increase the chances of completing a PPL course within a specific period, typically three or four weeks.

Several operators provide courses in France and Spain. The advantage that these offer over most of the American schools is that their courses lead to the granting of a JAR-FCL PPL, rather than an American Federal Aviation Administration (FAA) certificate, so you return fully qualified to fly in the UK. It is also possible on these courses to undertake the ground-school part of the course and take the technical examinations before going abroad to start the practical side of the syllabus, freeing more time for cramming those vital 45 flying hours into three weeks

The attractions of the USA for taking a PPL course are principally cost and weather. Flight training and aircraft hire are much cheaper in the USA than in the UK or mainland Europe, so it is possible for operators to offer packages that include ground and flight training, exams, accommodation, return airline fares and sometimes car hire for figures that may be below the cost of flight training alone at home. As a rule, the flight training element of such packages can cost around half that of the equivalent tuition in the UK.

US schools that are popular with overseas students tend to be located in the southern states, Florida being particularly popular because there is a good chance that the weather will be suitable for flying on most days. This ensures that rapid progress should be possible, and completion of the course is quite feasible within three or four weeks; perhaps less if you learn quickly. Pick the right school and instructor, enjoy good luck with the weather, and everything should go as advertised.

It may sound too good to be true, and there are drawbacks. In many cases, courses are for a US FAA licence, not a JAR-FCL PPL, although you can find American schools that offer training for this licence. If you opt for an FAA licence, you will need an FAA medical certificate before you go, but this can be acquired in Britain. A list of FAA Appointed Medical Examiners can be obtained from the FAA office at Sipson Court, 595 Sipson Road, Sipson, West Drayton, Middlesex, UB7 OJD. Requests for the list should be made in writing to the above address, or by fax on 0208 754 8826, but *not* by telephone. Your FAA PPL can be validated for use in the UK when you return home, and you may continue to fly quite legally. However, the FAA requires pilots to take a biennial review, which means that you will either have to seek out a UK-based FAA designated instructor (and there are some) or return to the USA for your check ride when the time comes around.

The alternative, which is probably wiser, bearing in mind that American and British air traffic control systems and operating procedures differ considerably, that our airspace is generally much more congested and restricted, and that the clear blue skies of Florida are no preparation for British weather, is to convert your FAA PPL to a JAR one upon your return. The CAA is prepared to do this, provided you can meet certain requirements. First, you must send in the FAA Temporary Airman Certificate, which will have been issued by your examiner in the USA, your medical certificate, log book and a fee for assessment by the Flight Crew Licensing Branch at Gatwick Airport. If all is well, and you have logged a minimum of 100 hours, you must then sit the UK air law, human performance and limitations, and communications examinations, take an RT test, take the PPL Skill Test and pay for the issue of your British licence. If you have logged fewer than 100 hours, but do meet the experience requirements of the JAR-FCL PPL, you will be required to complete all the ground examinations, as well as taking the RT and skill tests. Ground tuition at a UK school will probably be necessary preparation for the examinations and tests. You would be wise also to take some dual flying instruction to familiarize yourself with UK procedures. If you plan to hire aircraft from a British club or school, they will almost certainly require this anyway. All of this will add to the cost of obtaining your PPL in the USA, but it does give you valid licences for both countries – a great asset if you plan to take holidays or do further training in America. Of course, if you opt for a school that offers JAR training, you should not have these problems.

While most operators offering package courses abroad are honest and endeavour to provide a good service, there have been sorry instances of students finding themselves having to pay substantially for hidden 'extras' after arriving in the USA, or discovering that promised accommodation or training was not up to standard. As most of these operators require full payment in advance of your travelling to the USA, you would be well advised to make careful enquiries of any school whose offers you are tempted to accept. At the very least, ask for a list of satisfied British students who have trained at the school, and contact them for their experiences. If a school cannot, or will not, provide such a list, go elsewhere. Also check exactly what you are getting for your money. Are state taxes, examination fees and insurance indemnity included? If car hire is offered, does it include the cost of a collision damage waiver?

Some courses guarantee to that you will obtain your licence for the quoted fee, no matter how many flying hours it takes. However, if you fail to complete the course in the three weeks or whatever period you have booked, you will have to bear the cost of flying back to America at some future date to finish it. On this point, remember that to obtain your Temporary Airman Certificate, you must pass the written examinations before leaving the UK, and the results can take some time to come through, unless the exams are taken at an FAA exam centre that uses a computer-based testing system providing 'instant' results. In addition, there is a thirty-day wait to re-sit failed parts of an exam, although this can be, and often is, waived. You must also pass your check ride or practical test (equivalent to the JAR Skill Test), after which the Temporary Airman Certificate is issued by the examiner. Without written and check-ride passes, you will come home with no more than some good flying experience.

Since the air fares included in package courses are usually on non-amendable tickets, you will either have to fly back again at your own expense, or stay on and bear the cost of a one-way air ticket to complete the course.

The prospect of learning to fly in clear blue skies and warm sunshine, with sandy beaches nearby may seem attractive, but remember that becoming a pilot, particularly in as short a period as three or four weeks, will be hard work, and there is unlikely to be much time for anything other than studying, flying, eating and sleeping. Wherever you choose to learn to fly, it should be enjoyable, but do not expect it to be a relaxing holiday.

Another 'overseas' possibility, much closer to home, is training in the Channel Islands. There, training is free of VAT, and there are lower rates of duty on aviation fuel, so it is possible to learn to fly there for less than at some schools in mainland Britain. Operators on Guernsey and Jersey offer residential courses for the JAR-FCL PPL and ratings, and provide various grades of accommodation as desired. Their PPL courses generally last three or four weeks and include ground school.

MOVING UP

As we have seen, the PPL is a minimum qualification. Its scope can be greatly expanded as experience grows by a number of additional ratings, which are described briefly here.

Night Qualification

A private pilot who possesses only a basic PPL cannot legally fly as pilot-in-command after dark. For post-sunset flight, a JAR-FCL PPL Night Qualification is required. The rating allows flight with passengers, but, as with the carriage of passengers during daylight, it is subject to a recency rule.

The issue of the rating requires a PPL holder to have completed 5 hours of night flying. Three of those hours must be dual night flying instruction,

Practically all PPL training is carried out on aircraft with nosewheel landing gear. Before a tailwheel aircraft, such as this Luscombe Silvaire, can be flown, however, a pilot must undergo differences training on that type of aircraft. Other features that require such training include retractable landing gear, variable-pitch propeller, turbocharged engine and cabin pressurization. (Adrian Pingstone)

Private Pilot Licence – Night Qualification		
PPL(A)	5hr night flight time	3hr dual instruction in night flying
		1hr of night navigation instruction
		5 solo take-offs and landings at night

including 1 hour of night navigation. In addition, the applicant must have completed five solo take-offs and landings at night. The rating is non-expiring, but to carry passengers you must have made one take-off and landing while exclusively in control of the aircraft, at night, within the preceding ninety days.

You can train for a Night Qualification after gaining your PPL or while training for the licence. However, in the latter case, the time spent on night training cannot be considered as part of the minimum 45 hours required for the PPL.

A Night Qualification is also available to holders of a PPL(H), but the training/experience requirements are somewhat different. You cannot apply for a Night Qualification until you have gained 100 hours of flight time in helicopters – after obtaining your PPL. This should include 60 hours as PIC and 20 hours of cross-country flight. To obtain the Night Qualification, it is necessary to undergo 5 hours of theoretical knowledge instruction, 10 hours of dual instrument instruction (in addition to the hours completed for the PPL) and 5 hours of night training, 3 hours of which must be dual instruction. You should also complete five solo night circuits, each to include a take-off and landing. This course of training must be completed within a period of six months.

IMC Rating

The abbreviation IMC stands for instrument meteorological conditions, weather conditions that require a pilot to fly by reference to the aircraft's instruments rather than by external visual clues. As we have seen, the basic PPL restricts the holder to operating within sight of the earth's surface and to a minimum flight visibility for flight without passengers outside controlled airspace. The PPL syllabus provides a measure of instrument flying instruction, which is aimed at giving a student limited ability to control the aircraft and to perform simple manoeuvres by sole reference to instruments. This training, however, is no more than basic insurance against inadvertently entering cloud or poor weather conditions, in the hope that it will enable the pilot to retain control while returning to a point where visual reference to the ground can be regained. The IMC Rating is the minimum qualification for private pilots seeking to operate in instrument meteorological conditions, although it does not give a free hand to fly on the airways system or in controlled airspace, for which a full Instrument Rating (*see* later) is normally required. Exercising the privileges of the rating is also restricted to UK airspace only. It is not recognized in any other country, and is a rating exclusively available to the holders of JAR-FCL PPLs issued in the UK.

The IMC Rating dates from the period before harmonization of flight crew licensing in Europe, and since then there has always been a question mark hanging over its future. There is much opposition to the national rating elsewhere in Europe, where many consider that a full Instrument Rating is essential to fly in IMC. Although the rating continues to be available to UK licence holders as of early 2008, the European Aviation Safety Agency (EASA), which has assumed responsibility for flight crew licensing throughout Europe, has indicated that the rating will only remain valid until 2012. In the meantime, proponents of the rating, among them the CAA, have an opportunity to convince the rule-makers of its value. EASA has stated that it is determined to find a European solution to the problem, so it is possible that we may see a Euro-IMC Rating as a result. It is to be hoped that that will be the case, as you would be hard pushed to find a British pilot, instructor or examiner who believes the rating should be dropped.

To qualify for an IMC Rating, a pilot must have logged a minimum of 25 hours flying in aircraft after being issued with a PPL, of which at least 10 hours must have been as PIC, including no fewer than 5 hours on point-to-point cross-country flights, and must hold a valid RT licence. The IMC Rating course consists of a minimum of 15 hours of dual instrument flying training, of which 2 hours may be conducted in a simulator and 10 hours must be by sole reference to instruments; a ground training course; a written examination and a flight test.

Although the IMC Rating may not be issued until the minimum experience qualifications have been met, the flight and ground-school courses may be taken in advance, and some students do proceed directly to the IMC Rating course upon completion of their PPL training.

The flight training syllabus for the IMC Rating consists of a Basic Stage, comprising instrument appreciation, and basic and intermediate flight manoeuvres on instruments, with limited and partial panel flight, and the Applied Stage, which covers pre-flight planning, departure and en-route flying, instrument let-downs and approaches, and bad-weather circuits and landings. The Flight Test, which lasts for approximately 1½ hours, requires

IMC Rating – Aircraft (exclusively a UK CAA rating)		
PPL plus 25hr experience	10hr pilot-in-command	5hr cross-country
RT licence	15hr IMC instruction	2hr may be on a simulator

the pilot to demonstrate the ability to navigate on radio aids while flying solely by reference to instruments, to make a pilot-interpreted instrument approach, and to show the ability to use a second type of instrument approach aid, either pilot or ground-controller interpreted. The full syllabus is detailed in *LASORS*.

The IMC Rating is valid for a period of twenty-five months after a successful Flight Test, which may be completed in more than one flight, but not more than three, and the entire test must be completed within a twenty-eight-day period. The ground training syllabus, for which a minimum of twenty hours of study are recommended, covers physiological factors, aircraft flight instruments, the use of Aeronautical Information Publications, flight planning and the privileges of the IMC Rating. The written examination consists of one paper, which includes questions covering the planning and execution of a typical flight under instrument flight rules (IFR) operating outside controlled airspace. The flight test and written examination must be passed within the twelve months preceding an application for the rating, but there is no maximum duration for the course of instruction, although a concentrated IMC Rating course should last between six and eight days.

To maintain the validity of an IMC Rating, it is necessary to undergo a Revalidation Flight Test with an authorized examiner.

Multi-Engine Aircraft

In its basic form, the JAR-FCL PPL with SEP Rating covers only single-engine landplanes. To be able to fly as PIC of a multi-engine aircraft, another rating is required. In practice, 'multi-engine aircraft' mostly means twin-engine machines. However, it is not simply a matter of learning how to handle two sets of engine controls and instruments. Invariably, multi-engine aircraft are more complex than single-engine machines. Most offer higher performance and feature a greater variety of options in terms of loading, range and take-off/landing performance than a single-engine aircraft. In particular, the handling and performance characteristics of a twin-engine machine flying on one engine require training and practice if the advantages of two engines are to be exploited safely.

Prior to the harmonization of flight crew licensing in Europe, the CAA issued a single, simple Multi-Engine Rating for aircraft of up to 5,700kg. Under JAR-FCL, there are several ratings based on multi-pilot and multi-engine aircraft. For the limited scope of this book, however, we will restrict our interest to the Multi-Engine Piston (Land) Class Rating (Single Pilot).

To obtain the rating, a PPL holder requires 70 hours as pilot-in-command of single-engine aircraft and must have completed an approved course. The latter comprises a minimum of 2½ hours of dual instruction under normal multi-engine operating conditions, and 3½ hours of dual instruction in engine-failure procedures and asymmetric flight techniques. In addition, the student must undergo at least 7 hours of theoretical knowledge instruction on multi-engine aircraft operation. That is followed by a written examination, for which the pass mark is seventy-five per cent, and a Licensing Skill Test (LST) with an authorized examiner. The flight test includes normal flight procedures applicable to the PPL Skill Test, plus specific emergency procedures relating to multi-engine aircraft. The final flight test must be completed within six months of finishing the course.

The rating is valid for one year, and must be revalidated by undergoing a proficiency check with an authorized examiner and showing evidence of completing at least ten route sectors in a multi-engine aircraft within the validity period of the rating. If the experience requirements cannot be met, one route sector (a take-off, departure, cruise of not less than 15 minutes, arrival, approach and landing) must be completed with the examiner.

The Instrument Rating (Aeroplanes)

Qualification for the Instrument Rating (IR) requires the candidate to hold a PPL or a Commercial Pilot Licence (CPL) with a Night Qualification. Either must have logged 50 hours of cross-country flying as pilot-in-command (up to 40 hours in helicopters can count toward this) and must have passed an approved course of flight instruction. For single-engine

Instrument Rating – Aeroplanes			
	Up to 40hr cross-country experience may be as pilot-in command in helicopters		
Approved Course PPL(A) and Night Qualification *or* CPL(A) and Night Qualification 50hr cross-country experience plus approved instruction	50hr approved instruction for single-engine IR for PPL holders *or* 45hr instruction for single-engine IR for CPL holders *or* 50hr instruction for multi-engine IR for CPL holders *or* 55hr instruction for multi-engine IR for PPL holders	Up to 20hr may be flight trainer or 35hr flight simulator for single-engine IR *or* 25hr may be flight trainer or 40hr flight simulator for multi-engine IR	For a multi-engine IR, at least 15hr of instrument flight instruction must be in multi-engine aircraft

aircraft, this entails 50 hours for a PPL holder, or 45 hours for a CPL holder. Twenty hours of this may be ground instrument time in a flight trainer, or 35 hours in a flight simulator. Five additional hours of flight training apply if the qualification is for a multi-engine IR, and the ground-time allowance also increases by 5 hours, but at least 15 hours of the total training time must be flown in a multi-engine aircraft. Holders of a Helicopter IR may have the amount of flight training reduced to 10 hours.

An approved course of theoretical training of at least 250 hours must be completed within eighteen months, and the flying training certificated by the passing of a Skill Test within the period of validity of the pass in theoretical examinations. The number of attempts and treatment of failures for the Skill Test is the same as for the PPL Skill Test detailed previously in this chapter.

The theoretical-knowledge examinations cover the following subjects:

- Air Law and Operational Procedures.
- Aircraft General Knowledge.
- Human Performance and Limitations.
- Meteorology.
- Navigation.
- Communications (IFR).

The pass mark for all the examinations is seventy-five per cent.

Instrument Rating – Helicopters		
Single-Engine PPL(H) plus Night Qualification and 50hr cross-country experience plus 50hr instruction *or* CPL(H) plus Night Qualification and 45hr cross-country experience plus 50hr instruction	At least 10hr in helicopters	
	50hr instrument flight instruction	Up to 20hr may be in an approved flight trainer or up to 35hr in an approved flight simulator
Multi-Engine PPL(H) plus Night Qualification and 55hr cross-country experience plus 50hr instruction *or* CPL(H) plus Night Qualification and 50hr cross-country experience plus 50hr instruction	At least 15hr in multi-engine helicopters	
	55hr instrument flight instruction	Up to 20hr may be in an approved flight trainer or up to 40hr in an approved flight simulator
		At least 10hr must be in multi-engine helicopters

The Instrument Rating (Helicopters)

The requirements for a Helicopter IR are very similar to those for fixed-wing aircraft, but the break-down of the hours is slightly different. Exemption from the entire training course is granted to PPL(A) IR holders and some qualified service personnel.

Applicants for a Helicopter IR must hold a PPL(H) with a Night Qualification or a CPL(H), and must have completed at least 50 hours of cross-country flight time as PIC in helicopters or fixed-wing aircraft, of which at least 10 hours must be in helicopters. For single-engine helicopters, an approved training course of 50 hours of instrument flying instruction must then be undertaken. Of the 50 hours, up to 20 hours may be instrument ground time in an approved flight and navigation trainer, or up to 35 hours in an approved flight simulator. At least 10 hours must be in a single-engine helicopter. If the rating is for a multi-engine helicopter, the total hours are increased to 55, up to 20 of which can be in a trainer or 40 hours in a simulator. At least 10 hours must be in a multi-engine helicopter. Five hours can be allowed off the total training hours if the applicant holds a CPL(H). The training course culminates in a Skill Test.

The Skill Test is a flight test similar to that required for fixed-wing aircraft. The candidate may fail and retake one section, but if any section is failed on the retest, the whole test must be taken again. If two or more sections are failed, the entire test must be taken again. All parts of the skill test must be completed and passed within six months. The theoretical-knowledge examinations are the same as those listed for the PPL(A) IR.

ANY QUESTIONS?

To round off this chapter, here are the answers to some questions that may be in your mind.

I have done some gliding. Will it help with a PPL?

Under the JAR-FCL PPL rules, holders of pilot licences or equivalent privileges for gliders, self-sustaining gliders, self-launching gliders, helicopters and three-axis microlights may be credited with a total of ten per cent of their total flight time as pilot-in-command, up to a maximum of ten hours toward a JAR-FCL PPL(A).

Are there any sponsorship schemes?

Earlier editions of this book carried details of as many as six sponsorship schemes for the PPL. Sadly, today, there are fewer organizations that offer financial assistance toward a PPL. However, the Guild of Air Pilots and Air Navigators (GAPAN) annually awards several full PPL courses. Applicants must be at least seventeen years old, able to qualify for a JAR Class 2 medical certificate and be available to train during the summer. Applications should be made by early April, and in the first instance, you need to complete an application form (which can be downloaded from the GAPAN web site or obtained by post), giving brief personal details, previous flying experience and the reason for wanting to obtain a PPL. Potential candidates will be called for interview in London, and training usually takes place in July at a school of GAPAN's choice.

The British Women Pilots' Association also operates a PPL scholarship scheme that is open to women only.

Another ray of sunshine is the International Air Tattoo Flying Scholarship for disabled people. This is awarded in memory of the late Sir Douglas Bader, and partly sponsored by King Abdullah of Jordan. The scheme annually provides forty hours of flying experience on totally funded, six-week residential courses in South Africa for physically handicapped applicants aged over seventeen years. In addition, ten-hour mini-courses are awarded at Goodwood Flying School in West Sussex. In the first instance, you need to complete an application form, which you can do online, or you can e-mail, write or telephone for one.

In addition, the Air League offers a number of full and partial sponsorships for young men and women between the ages of seventeen and twenty-six to help them gain NPPLs, while the Royal Aero Club offers £500 bursaries to those aged between sixteen and twenty-one to help them further their interest in aviation. This can include flying training.

Full contact details for the organizations listed above can be found in Chapter 6.

Although it is not a direct form of flying sponsorship, many youngsters have taken jobs with flying clubs and schools under various youth training schemes, and thereby learned to fly and gained their PPLs. Obviously, such opportunities are limited, but they are definitely worth investigating.

I do not want to become a pilot, but I fly as a passenger and would like to learn enough to take over in an emergency.
That is very wise. What you need is a Second Pilot or Safety Pilot's course (it is called a 'Pinch Hitter's' course in the USA). Many flying schools offer such training, which usually consists of 6–10 hours of dual flying training and 10–20 hours of ground school. This covers aircraft handling, basic navigation and use of the aircraft radio.

Although such a course does not earn the student a licence or an official rating, it does offer two major worthwhile benefits. From the safety aspect, the student should, in most circumstances, be able to land the aircraft in which he or she is travelling without injury to the aircraft or occupants. However, the more appreciated benefit will be from the additional satisfaction of knowing what is happening during the flight, removing the mystery of dials and buttons in the cockpit.

This type of course is a sensible 'must' for regular passengers, but be warned: many people who intend taking just the safety course catch the bug and go on to complete the entire PPL course.

CHAPTER 3
THE NATIONAL
PRIVATE PILOT
LICENCE

For many pilots, simply being airborne on a beautiful sunny day is an end in itself. They do not need, or want, to fly large and complex aircraft, or to fly in cloud, at night or overseas. Their flying is purely recreational, and it is for such pilots that the National Private Pilot Licence (NPPL) was introduced in the UK in 2002. It is a basic pilot's licence that does have restrictions in the privileges it conveys, but it is a much simpler licence to obtain than a PPL, which makes it an attractive proposition for many. It is also a UK-only licence that falls outside the JAR system and, as such, is not recognized (at present) outside the UK. Because of this, it cannot be used as a stepping-stone toward a JAR-FCL commercial licence, unlike the PPL. If required, however, it can be converted to a PPL with additional training.

Although the NPPL is issued by the CAA, regulation of the NPPL licensing system has been devolved to a number of recreational flying organizations. These are:

- Aircraft Owners and Pilots Association (AOPA).
- Light Aircraft Association (LAA).
- British Microlight Aircraft Association (BMAA).
- British Gliding Association (BGA).

Together, these organizations operate the National Pilots Licensing Group, which is responsible for overseeing the system. Contact details for this group and its constituent organizations can be found in Chapter 6.

The holder of an NPPL is restricted to flight by day, in good weather and in single-engine aircraft with no more than four seats. Ratings can be added to the licence to permit flight in particular classes of aircraft, such as Simple Single Engine Aircraft (SSEA – effectively the same as the PPL's SEP), Microlight, Self Launching Motor Glider (SLMG) and Powered Parachute. In fact, the NPPL has replaced the original stand-alone microlight licence and PPL(SLMG). The restrictions still allow a considerable variety of machines to be flown, including all the popular light training and touring aircraft. Provided suitable differences training is undertaken, these can include machines with retractable landing gear, variable-pitch propellers and cabin pressurization. However, there is no provision for instrument or multi-engine ratings, or for a helicopter NPPL.

MEDICAL REQUIREMENTS

One of the major attractions of the NPPL is its reduced medical requirement. Although a JAR-FCL Class 1 or Class 2 medical certificate would be acceptable for the issue of an NPPL, in fact all that is necessary is a declaration of medical fitness signed by the applicant and validated by his or her GP to prevent the concealment of disease. The criteria used for this are based on those employed by the Driving and Vehicle Licensing Agency (DVLA) for the issue of driving licences. Provided there is nothing in an applicant's medical history that would prevent him or her from meeting the standard required for a Group 2 professional driving licence, the declaration can be used to obtain an unrestricted NPPL, allowing the carriage of up to three passengers. If the Group 2 standard cannot be met, but the applicant's medical history is within the Group 1 (private driving licence) standard, a restricted NPPL can be obtained. This limits the holder to solo flight only, or flight with another qualified pilot, who must act as a safety pilot.

An advantage of this method of medical certification is that a GP has access to an applicant's medical records, and therefore is equipped to determine whether there is anything in the individual's medical history that might cause in-flight incapacitation at some point in the future. Such conditions do not always come to light during medical examinations for JAR-FCL licences.

Once the declaration has been countersigned by the GP and a copy sent to the relevant organization responsible for the type of flying to be pursued, it acts as a student pilot's licence, allowing the holder to fly solo. The minimum age for countersignature is one month before the applicant's sixteenth birthday, allowing solo flight at sixteen.

NPPL medical declarations must be renewed at certain intervals, depending on the applicant's age. A declaration remains current up to the age of forty-five, after which it must be renewed every five years up to the age of sixty-five. After that, it must be renewed annually. That said, it remains the responsibility of the holder to assess his or her own fitness continually, and to stop flying if any medical condition arises that could cause problems. This should be discussed with the GP, any doctor treating the condition or with an NPPL medical advisor.

TRAINING – SSEA/SLMG

As with a PPL, individuals can begin training for an NPPL at any age, but solo flight is not permitted until the student has reached the age of sixteen

The Diamond DA40 is one of many modern four-seat light aircraft that can be flown by the holder of an NPPL with SSEA rating. Built from modern composite materials, the aircraft has been offered in variants with fixed-pitch and constant-speed propellers, and with a diesel engine. The latest examples have an LCD flight instrument system – a 'glass cockpit'. (Adrian Pingstone)

(and has a countersigned medical declaration), while the licence itself cannot be issued until the applicant has reached the age of seventeen. The training requirement for an NPPL with an SSEA or SLMG rating is lower than that required for a PPL(A), at 32 hours minimum. For the SSEA rating, training must be carried out by a JAR-FCL qualified instructor at a CAA-registered facility or flight training organization. In effect, this means than any organization offering PPL training can also instruct for the NPPL. Training for the SLMG rating must be done at an approved BGA site.

The 32-hour course must comprise the following: 22 hours of dual instruction, which must include 1 hour of instrument appreciation; 10 hours of solo flight time, which must include 4 hours of cross-country flying, during which a flight of at least 100 nautical miles must be made with landings at two airfields other than the departure airfield. However, before this qualifying cross-country flight can be made, the student must take and pass a Navigation Skill Test (NST), which lasts for a minimum of an hour (this does not count toward the 32-hour requirement). Note that the 32-hour requirement is a minimum, and it is quite possible that more time will be required to reach the necessary level of competence. The training is based on the PPL syllabus and employs the same numbered exercises.

As of early 2008, students seeking to obtain an NPPL with either SSEA or SLMG rating were required to take and pass all the theoretical-knowledge examinations for the PPL(A), as described in Chapter 2. However, this situation may change in future, as there is an outline intention to simplify the examinations in line with the practical and relatively limited needs of the NPPL holder.

Once the NST has been passed, training completed and the theoretical-

Until the advent of the NPPL, pilots of self-launching motor gliders, like this Grob G109B, had to have a full PPL. In the NPPL with SLMG rating, they require less training, which can be carried out from recognized gliding sites. (Adrian Pingstone)

knowledge examinations passed, the student is ready to take the General Skill Test (GST), which must be flown within six months of completing the training. All sections of the test must be passed, but any sections that are failed may be retaken. There is no limit to the number of GSTs that an applicant may take.

Passing the GST leads to the issue of the NPPL, which is valid for life. However, the medical declaration must be renewed at the specified intervals, as detailed previously, and the rating (SSEA or SLMG) must be kept current to maintain the privileges conveyed by the licence. For the SSEA and SLMG class rating to be valid for any flight, the pilot must have flown no fewer than twelve hours in the previous twenty-four months, at least eight as PIC, with twelve take-offs and landings. Six of the twelve hours must have been flown in the previous twelve months. In addition, a flight with an authorized instructor of at least one hour's duration is required. Alternatively, the pilot can have undertaken a Skill Test with an authorized examiner in the previous twelve months. In addition, passengers may not be carried unless in the preceding ninety days, the pilot has made at least three take-offs and landings in sole charge of an aircraft in the same class as that being flown.

TRAINING – MICROLIGHTS

Although to many, the idea of a microlight aircraft may suggest a flimsy, open machine with a flapping, sail-type overhead wing, in fact many modern, three-axis microlights (machines with conventional ailerons, elevators and rudder) are virtually indistinguishable from their more conventional light aircraft counterparts. Modern manufacturing techniques and materials make it possible to build aircraft of conventional design, but low weight, thus qualifying them as microlights. To this end, aircraft must weigh no more than 300kg if single-seaters or 450kg if two-seaters.

The age and medical requirements for an NPPL (Microlights) are the same as for the SSEA and SLMG class ratings. However, the experience and training requirements are lower than those required for heavier aircraft, and applicants may opt for a restricted or unrestricted licence. The former has certain operational limitations, some of which can be removed when the pilot has gained a certain amount of experience.

For an unrestricted NPPL (Microlights), applicants are required to complete 25 hours of training, 5 hours of which must be navigation training (to include 3 hours of solo cross-country flying and two flights of at least 40 nautical miles, during each of which a landing must be made at another site at least 15 nautical miles from the departure point); 10 hours must be as pilot-in-command and flown within nine months of applying for the licence. At the completion of the training, students are required to take and pass a General Flight Test (GFT). In addition, applicants must take and pass the following theoretical-knowledge ground examinations:

- Aviation Law, Flight Rules and Procedures.
- Human Performance and Limitations.
- Navigation and Meteorology.
- Aircraft (General)
- Aircraft (Type) - an oral test carried out during the GFT.

The NPPL with Microlight rating has replaced the original microlight pilot licence. Many modern microlights have three-axis controls (ailerons, elevators and rudder) and look like conventional light aircraft. This is an Aeroprakt A22 Foxbat, a Russian design that falls within the 450kg maximum weight limit for a two-seater. A 100hp engine ensures good performance. (Adrian Pingstone)

A restricted NPPL (Microlights) has lower experience/training requirements than the unrestricted licence. Students must undergo a minimum of 15 hours of training, no fewer than 7 hours of which must be as pilot-in-command and flown in the nine months preceding the date of licence application. In addition, the theoretical-knowledge ground examinations listed previously must be taken and passed, as must a GFT.

The restricted licence only permits flight within the UK, the Channel Islands and the Isle of Man, when the surface wind speed is 15kt or less, there is no cloud below 1,000ft above ground level, and the in-flight visibility is at least 10km. Furthermore, flights may not be beyond an 8-nautical-mile radius of the take-off site, nor be at night, nor pass over any congested area of a town or city. A passenger may not be carried, unless he or she is a qualified flying instructor and the machine has dual controls. This last restriction may be removed after the pilot has completed 25 hours of flying, at least 10 hours of which must be as pilot-in-command. The wind speed/cloud/visibility and flight-radius restrictions can also be removed when the pilot has completed 25 hours of microlight flying and undertaken 5 hours of navigation instruction, as for the unrestricted licence.

The NPPL (Microlights) is issued for life, but it has the same experience requirements to maintain the rating as the SSEA and SLMG class ratings.

THE FUTURE

One drawback of the NPPL is that it is restricted to the UK and to UK registered aircraft. You cannot take this licence abroad on holiday with you and fly foreign-registered aircraft, or take a UK-registered light aircraft abroad, although this may be possible with microlights if written permission is obtained from the relevant authority. At the time of writing, there is talk that it may be recognized in France at some future date.

However, it may be that the NPPL's days are numbered. There is a proposal to adopt a Light Aircraft Pilot Licence (LAPL) within the European Union, which will be valid for simple aircraft below 2,000kg and have similar medical requirements to the UK NPPL. As of early 2008, this licence was in the planning stage and there was no indication of when it is likely to be introduced. When that day comes, though, it is difficult to see how the NPPL will continue, especially in its SSEA and SLMG forms. The new LAPL will be issued under the auspices of the European Aviation Safety Agency (EASA), which has assumed overall responsibility for pilot licensing within the EU.

Chapter 4
The Commercial
Pilot

As explained in Chapter 2, the PPL is strictly an amateur qualification, entitling you to fly for personal business or pleasure. The JAR define a private pilot as 'A pilot who holds a licence which prohibits the piloting of aircraft in operations in which renumeration is given'. To receive payment for your services as a pilot, a professional qualification is a legal requirement.

In the UK, there are two grades of professional flying licence: the Commercial Pilot Licence (CPL) and the Airline Transport Pilot Licence (ATPL). The minimum experience requirements for these (as of early 2008) are given in this chapter, but since requirements and licence privileges can change, readers are advised to consult the CAA publication *LASORS* or visit the CAA web site for the latest information on all professional licensing matters. There are approximately 16,000 holders of professional pilot licences in the UK; 4,000 of them are CPLs and 12,000 ATPLs.

THE COMMERCIAL PILOT LICENCE

The Commercial Pilot Licence is the basic professional flying licence, and it permits the holder to act as pilot-in-command of aircraft certificated for single-pilot operation in carrying out what is termed aerial work. This includes flying instruction, aerial photography, banner towing and carrying passengers on local flights (pleasure flights) of no more than 50 nautical miles under Visual Flight Rules (VFR) that return to the departure airfield. A CPL holder with more than 500 hours of flight time may carry passengers over greater distances and land at other airfields, but only under VFR.

The minimum age for applicants for a JAR-FCL CPL (Aeroplanes) is eighteen years, and they must hold a JAR-FCL Class 1 medical certificate. The examination for the latter is more stringent than for a Class 2 certificate, and the initial examination must be carried out by a CAA doctor at the authority's Gatwick headquarters (subsequent examinations for revalidation can be carried out by a CAA-approved doctor). Although no formal educational qualifications are required to train for a CPL, or an ATPL, a good grounding in mathematics and physics will prove invaluable in coping with the theoretical-knowledge requirements for the ground exams.

The Piper Seneca series of twin-engine aircraft has been popular with flying schools offering commercial pilot courses. It was derived from the single-engine PA-32. This example is a Seneca II. (Adrian Pingstone)

There are two types of approved course: integrated and modular. The integrated course for the JAR-FCL CPL is full-time and can last between nine and twenty-four months. Courses are available for training from *ab initio* right up to issue of the CPL, or they can be tailored to existing PPL holders. In the latter case, fifty per cent of the hours flown prior to the course can be credited against the required flight instruction for the CPL, up to a maximum of 40 hours, or 45 hours if a night flying qualification is held. Graduates of an integrated course must have completed a minimum of 150 hours of flight time, excluding type-rating training. Of that total flight time, 80 hours must be dual instruction (up to 5 hours may be ground instrument instruction); 70 hours must be as pilot-in-command; 20 hours must be cross-country flight time as pilot-in-command (including one VFR flight of at least 300 nautical miles, landing at two airfields other than the departure airfield); 5 hours must be dual instruction in a complex type of aircraft with variable-pitch propeller and retractable landing gear, 5 hours must be night flying (including 3 hours dual, 1 hour cross-country, and five solo take-offs and landings), and 10 hours must be instrument flight instruction, 5 hours of which may be in a ground trainer or simulator. The theoretical training comprises at least 300 hours of instruction, but this is reduced to 200 hours for PPL holders. As with the PPL, it is necessary to take and pass a number of theoretical-knowledge examinations before attempting the final Skill Test for the issue of the licence. Examinations are held in the following subjects:

- Air Law.
- Navigation.

- Aircraft General Knowledge.
- Operational Procedures.
- Flight Performance and Planning.
- Principles of Flight.
- Human Performance and Limitations.
- Communications (VFR).
- Meteorology.

The pass mark for all the examinations is seventy-five per cent, and they must be completed within an eighteen-month period. The pass is valid for a period of thirty-six months for the issue of a CPL.

Having completed the training course and passed the ground examinations, the student undergoes the final Skill Test with an authorized examiner. As with the PPL, failure of more than one section of the test means having to take the entire test again, but if only one section is failed, it can be taken again. However, a further failure will lead to the entire test having to be flown. There is no limit to the number of Skill Tests that can be attempted, and once a pass is achieved, it is valid for twelve months for the issue of a CPL.

The modular course is aimed at PPL holders who cannot afford, or do not wish to commit to a full-time integrated course. Undertaking a modular course allows the student to work at his or her own pace, completing the approved modules of training over a period of time, which can provide

The Cessna Citation Mustang is one of a new breed of very light jet (VLJ), which is likely to be gracing the training fleets of the major commercial pilot flying schools before long, providing jet training at an early stage. Powered by two Pratt & Whitney turbofan engines, it has seating for two crew and four passengers. (Cessna Aircraft Company)

Commercial Pilot Licence (CPL and CPL/IR) – Aeroplanes		
Integrated Course CPL 150hr flight time	10hr may be instrument ground time	
	20hr may be in helicopters and/or touring motorgliders	
	70hr as PIC	
	20hr of cross-country as PIC	Including a cross-country flight of at least 300 nautical miles, landing at two different aerodromes
	10hr instrument instruction time	Up to 5hr may be instrument ground time
	5hr night flight time	
Integrated Course CPL/IR 180hr flying training	Up to 10hr may be instrument ground time	
	70hr PIC	20hr instrument flight time as student pilot-in-command (SPIC)
	50hr cross-country flight as PIC	Including a cross-country flight of at least 300 nautical miles landing at two different aerodromes
	70hr of instrument flight instruction	Up to 10hr may be ground time in a flight trainer or simulator
		20hr as SPIC
	5hr of night flying	Five solo take-offs and full-stop landings
		3hr dual instruction including 1hr night navigation

financial savings. To take the modular course, an applicant needs to be a PPL holder with at least 150 hours of flight time (*see* table), and this reduces the required amount of flight instruction to 25 hours dual, of which 10 hours must be instrument instruction, although 5 of those hours may be in a ground trainer or simulator. At least 5 hours of instruction must be carried out on a complex aircraft with a variable-pitch propeller and retractable landing gear. Flight time on the course may be counted toward the total

Commercial Pilot Licence (CPL) – Aeroplanes		
Modular Course CPL 200hr flight time	150hr as PPL(A) prior experience	
	100hr as PIC	
	20hr of cross-country as PIC	Including a cross-country flight of at least 300 nautical miles landing at two different aerodromes
	25hr dual instruction (at least 5hr in a complex aircraft)	
	10hr instrument instruction	Up to 5hr may be instrument ground time
	5hr night flight time	

experience required for the issue of the CPL, which is a total of 200 hours under the modular course requirements, including 100 hours as pilot-in-command, 20 hours of cross-country flying (including one flight of 300 nautical miles with landings at two airfields other than the departure airfield), 10 hours instrument instruction (up to 5 hours may be in a ground trainer or simulator), and 5 hours of night flying (including 3 hours of dual instruction, 1 hour of cross-country navigation and five solo take-offs and landings). As with the integrated course, it is necessary to take and pass the CPL theoretical-knowledge examinations prior to attempting the Skill Test.

A useful extension to the CPL, and an essential one for decent employment prospects, is an Instrument Rating (IR). In addition to the privileges conferred by a CPL, the holder of a CPL/IR can also act as co-pilot in certain aircraft used for IFR public transport flights. These aircraft have a 5,700kg weight limit and include such machines as the de Havilland Twin Otter, Beech King Air and Embraer Bandeirante. A full-time integrated course is offered for the CPL/IR that can last between nine and thirty months. As with the basic CPL, the course may be from *ab initio* to completion, or allow for the possession of a PPL. In the latter case, the same 40- or 45-hour credit against the required flight instruction is offered. Students on the course must undergo a minimum of 180 hours of training. This must include 80 hours of dual instruction (40 hours of which may be instrument ground time), 100 hours as pilot-in-command (including 50 hours VFR and 50 hours instrument time), 50 hours of cross-country flight (including one flight of at least 300 nautical miles with landings at two airfields other than the departure airfield), 5 hours' night flying (including 3 hours of dual instruction, 1 hour of cross-country navigation, and five solo

The Beechcraft Super King Air 200 is typical of the type of twin-turboprop air taxi/corporate aircraft on which many newly qualified commercial pilots will find their first co-pilot position. (Adrian Pingstone)

take-offs and landings) and 100 hours of instrument time (50 hours dual and 50 hours as student-pilot-in-command). In addition to the CPL ground examinations, the student must also take and pass IR examinations in the following subjects:

- Air Law and Operational Procedures.
- Aircraft General Knowledge.
- Flight Performance and Planning.
- Human Performance and Limitations.
- Meteorology.
- Navigation.
- Communications (IFR).

The theoretical-knowledge syllabus comprises 500 hours of instruction. In addition to the CPL Skill Test, applicants for the CPL/IR must undergo a separate IR Skill Test with an authorized examiner.

Those individuals following the modular route can add a separate Instrument Rating to their licence when ready and able to do so; details of the rating are given in Chapter 2. In addition, further training modules, such as Multi-Engine, Crew Resource Management and Multi-Crew Co-operation, allow the student to progress steadily toward an Airline Transport Pilot Licence (ATPL).

In many cases, students seeking a CPL/IR do so on their way toward gaining an ATPL. In this case, it is usual to take the ATPL theoretical-knowledge examinations rather than those for the CPL/IR, which is a step toward what is known as a 'frozen ATPL'. Details of these examinations are given later in this chapter.

COMMERCIAL PILOT LICENCE – HELICOPTERS

So far we have been concerned with training on fixed-wing aircraft. However, the increasing importance of helicopters in commercial aviation makes a rotary-wing licence a valuable asset for a professional pilot. In 1968, there were just 136 civil helicopters registered in the UK; in 1998, there were 906; in 2008, there were 1,390.

The age, medical, ground-examination and flight-test requirements for a Commercial Pilot Licence (Helicopters) are similar to those for fixed-wing commercial licences. Under the JAR-FCL provisions, there are two routes to a CPL(H): by training on an approved, full-time integrated course or on an approved modular course. Whichever method is chosen, the applicant must

Commercial Pilot Licence – Helicopters			
Integrated Course 135hr flying training Includes 100hr dual instruction and 35hr PIC in helicopters	(a) 15hr may be in aircraft and/or touring motor gliders (b) Up to 10hr may be instrument ground time	10hr basic instrument flight instruction	5hr may be ground instrument time
		5hr night flying	3hr dual instruction, including 1hr night navigation
			Five solo circuits, take-offs and landings
		10hr cross-country flight totalling at least 100 nautical miles, in the course of which two landings at two different aerodromes are made	
Modular Course PPL(H) plus 155hr flight time and a Night Qualification	50hr PIC		
	10hr cross-country		
	Dual flight instruction	If no IR – 30hr including 10hr basic instrument training (up to 5hr can be ground instrument time)	
		If IR held – 20hr visual flight instruction including at least 5hr cross-country	

be at least eighteen years of age and must hold a valid JAR-FCL Class 1 medical certificate.

Candidates attending an integrated course (of between nine and twenty-four months) must receive a minimum of 135 hours of training. Those hours must include at least 100 hours of dual instruction; 35 hours as pilot-in-command; 10 hours of dual cross-country flying; 10 hours of cross-country flying as PIC, including a flight of at least 100 nautical miles with landings at two different aerodromes other than the departure aerodrome; 5 hours of night flying, including 3 hours of dual instruction, 1 hour of cross-country navigation, and five solo circuits with five take-offs and landings; and 10 hours of basic instrument flight instruction, of which up to 5 hours may be instrument ground time. Of the 100 hours of dual instruction, between 30 and 40 hours may be in a helicopter ground trainer or simulator, depending on type, and 20 hours may be in a fixed-wing aircraft.

Qualification under the modular course requires the applicant to hold a PPL(H), preferably with a Night Qualification. If the latter is not held, a minimum of 5 hours of night flight instruction will be added to the course. Prior to embarking on the course, the applicant should have logged at least 155 hours of flight time in helicopters, including 50 hours as PIC, of which 10 hours must be cross-country flight. Alternatively, if the applicant also holds a PPL(A), only 135 hours of helicopter flight time are required, 30 hours of which must be as PIC. If the applicant holds a CPL(A), only 105 hours of helicopter flight time are required. The modular course for applicants for a CPL(H) comprises at least 30 hours of dual flight instruction, including 10 hours of basic instrument training, of which up to 5 hours may be in an approved ground trainer or simulator, or a fixed-wing aircraft. Applicants with a valid Instrument Rating require only 20 hours of dual visual flight instruction, including at least 5 hours of cross-country flight.

Flight time amassed during the modular course counts toward the total experience required for issue of the licence, which is a minimum of 185 hours, including 50 hours as PIC, 10 hours of cross-country flight (including a flight of at least 100 nautical miles with landings at two airfields other than the departure airfield), 10 hours of instrument dual instruction time (of which up to 5 hours may be in a ground trainer or simulator) and 5 hours night flying (including 3 hours of dual instruction, 1 hour of cross-country navigation, and five circuits with five take-offs and landings). A holder of a PPL(A) is given a 20-hour credit against the 185-hour total, while 50 hours are credited if a CPL(A) is held.

Both routes to the CPL(H) culminate in a Skill Test, but before this can be undertaken, applicants must have completed a course of ground instruction at an approved flying training organization or at an organization specializing in theoretical-knowledge instruction, and taken and passed the ground examinations. The theoretical-knowledge training comprises 550 hours of instruction for *ab initio* students on the approved integrated course, or 500 hours for PPL holders. The examinations cover nine subjects:

- Air Law.
- Aircraft General Knowledge.
- Flight Performance and Planning.
- Human Performance and Limitations.
- Meteorology.
- Navigation.
- Operational Procedures.
- Principles of Flight.
- Communications (VFR).

A seventy-five per cent pass mark is required for each subject. The complete set of examinations must be passed within an eighteen-month period, and a pass will be accepted for the grant of the CPL(H) during the thirty-six months from the date of first gaining a pass.

As of early 2008, CAA-approved commercial helicopter pilot training courses were offered by only two operators: Cabair and Bristow Academy Inc., the latter being based in the USA (*see* Chapter 6), but at the time of writing, sponsorship was non-existent. Because operating costs of helicopters are so much higher than for fixed-wing aircraft, obtaining a CPL(H) without some form of sponsorship is probably prohibitive. Consequently, most commercial helicopter pilots tend to be ex-military. However, situations do change, and sponsorship may become available again in future.

For anyone thinking of a career in civil helicopter flying, an enquiry to the British Helicopter Advisory Board (*see* Chapter 6) would probably be as good a starting point as any, and first gaining a PPL(H) would improve one's admittedly limited chances of sponsorship to a commercial licence.

Moving up the scale, commercial pilots may find themselve working for regional airlines, flying turboprop airliners like this ATR 72. (Adrian Pingstone)

AIRLINE TRANSPORT PILOT LICENCE – AEROPLANES

This is the ultimate pilot's licence. An ATPL allows the holder to operate as pilot-in-command of any aircraft, subject to holding the relevant type rating. Under JAR-FCL rules, the minimum age is twenty-one years, and candidates must possess a Class 1 medical certificate. As with the CPL, there are two routes of training toward an ATPL: integrated and modular. In addition, candidates must have logged 1,500 hours of flight experience before the licence can be issued, even though they may have completed all the necessary training and theoretical-knowledge examinations. This gives rise to what is known as a 'frozen ATPL', whereby the candidate has gained a CPL/IR with Multi-Engine Rating and Multi-Crew Co-operation credit, and has passed the ATPL ground examinations, but has yet to build sufficient hours to qualify for the issue of the licence. As such, the holder of the 'frozen ATPL' can act as the co-pilot of multi-pilot, multi-engine aircraft in commercial air transportation. The required experience must include the following minimum amounts:

- 500 hours of multi-pilot operations.
- 250 hours as pilot-in-command, which can include 150 hours as co-pilot (P2) acting as pilot-in-command under supervision (PIC/US) of a pilot-in-command.
- 200 hours of cross-country flight time, including 100 hours as PIC or PIC/US.
- 75 hours instrument time, which can include 30 hours in a ground trainer or simulator.
- 100 hours of night flying as PIC, PIC/US or P2.

The balance of the hours may be made up as follows:

- Any PIC/solo time counted in full.
- Any pilot-under-instruction (dual) time counted in full.
- Any PIC/US time counted in full.
- Any P2 time counted in full.
- Any student-pilot-in-command (SPIC) time counted in full up to a maximum of 50 hours toward the ATPL PIC time.
- Up to 100 hours in an aircraft flight simulator (25 hours of which may be in a navigation trainer).
- Up to 30 hours in a touring motor glider (TMG) or glider.

Up to fifty per cent of the 1,500 hours (and fifty per cent of each of the minimum experience requirements listed above) may be in helicopters. A further allowance is made for the holder of a Flight Engineer Licence, fifty per cent of the flight engineer time, up to a maximum of 250 hours, being

Airline Transport Pilot Licence – Aeroplanes			
Experience required: 1,500hr of flight time	250hr PIC	Up to 150hr as co-pilot acting as PIC	
	500hr in multi-pilot operations		
	Up to 100hr may be in a flight simulator		
	200hr cross-country	At least 100hr must be as PIC	
	100hr night flying		
	75hr instrument flight time		
ATPL Approved Integrated Course Provides qualification of a CPL(A) with Instrument Rating and to co-pilot on multi-pilot, multi-engine aircraft in commercial air transportation 195hr flying training (hours can form a combined function)	Up to 55hr instrument ground time		
	100hr as PIC	50hr VFR flight	
		50hr instrument flight as SPIC	
	50hr cross-country as PIC	Including a cross-country flight of at least 300 nautical miles, landing at two different aerodromes	
	5hr night flight	Five solo take-offs and full-stop landings	
		3hr dual instruction	
		1hr night navigation	
	115hr of instrument flight time	50hr instrument flight instruction	Up to 25hr instrument ground time in a flight trainer
			Up to 40hr in an approved flight simulator
		50hr as student PIC	
		15hr multi-crew co-operation	May all be simulator time

For many commercial pilots, the goal is an ATPL and the flight deck of an airliner like this Boeing 747-400. It can be a long and hard road, but for those who persevere, the outcome can be very rewarding. (Adrian Pingstone)

credited against the total of 1,500 hours and 500 hours multi-pilot time.

As with the CPL, the ATPL integrated course may take students from *ab initio* level to the 'frozen ATPL'. The course includes training to, and the issue of, a CPL(A)/IR with a Multi-Engine Class Rating and Multi-Crew Co-operation credit. For existing PPL(A) holders, fifty per cent of the hours flown by the entrant before embarking on the course may be credited toward the course flight time, up to a maximum of 40 hours experience, or 45 hours if a night flying qualification is held. Of those, 20 hours can be dual instruction. All of the required hours must be completed before the final ATPL Skill Test may be taken.

The ATPL integrated course, which can last between twelve and thirty-six months, comprises 195 hours of flying training, which must include the following minimums:

- 95 hours of dual instruction, of which up to 55 hours may be ground instrument instruction.
- 100 hours as PIC, of which 50 hours must be VFR and 50 hours instrument time.
- 50 hours of cross-country flying as pilot-in-command (including a flight of 300 nautical miles with landings at two airfields other than the departure airfield).
- 5 hours of night flying (including 3 hours of dual instruction, 1 hour of cross-country navigation, and five solo take-offs and landings).
- 50 hours of instrument instruction (of which 25 or 40 hours may be in a ground trainer or simulator, depending on type).

- 50 hours of instrument flight as student-pilot-in-command.
- 15 hours of multi-crew co-operation, which may be in a ground-based flight simulator.

In addition, the integrated course includes 750 hours of theoretical-knowledge instruction for the ground examinations, all of which must be completed within the same continuous approved course. The subjects are broken down into fourteen papers as follows:

- Air Law.
- Aircraft General Knowledge (two papers).
- Flight Performance and Planning (three papers).
- Human Performance and Limitations.
- Meteorology.
- Navigation (two papers).
- Operational Procedures.
- Principles of Flight.
- Communications (two papers).

Applicants taking the modular route also require the theoretical-knowledge qualifications, and they must be attained by taking a modular Airline Transport Pilot Theoretical Knowledge Course at an approved training organization. A minimum qualification of a PPL(A) is required prior to taking the course, which involves 650 hours of instruction. The course must be completed within a period of eighteen months. A pass in the examinations is valid for seven years from the last validity date of the Instrument Rating issued for the ATPL, allowing time for the necessary flight experience to be gained prior to issue of the licence.

AIRLINE TRANSPORT PILOT LICENCE – HELICOPTERS

As with fixed-wing aircraft, there are two routes to a JAR-FCL ATPL (Helicopters): either by training on an approved full-time integrated course or by taking modules of training over a period of time, progressing from PPL(H) to a CPL(H), then adding Instrument and Multi-Engine ratings, and undergoing Multi-Crew Co-operation training. Either way, the holder must be at least twenty-one years of age and must hold a valid JAR-FCL Class 1 medical certificate. In addition, candidates must have logged at least 1,000 hours of helicopter flight time before the licence can actually be issued. The required experience must include the following minimum amounts:

- 350 hours of multi-pilot operations.
- 250 hours as pilot-in-command, which can include 150 hours as co-pilot acting as PIC under supervision (PIC/US) of a PIC.

- 200 hours of cross-country flight time, which must include 70 hours as PIC or PIC/US.
- 70 hours of instrument time, which can include 30 hours of instrument ground time.
- 100 hours of night flying as PIC, PIC/US or co-pilot (P2).

The balance of the hours may be made up as follows:

- Any PIC/solo time counted in full.
- Any pilot-under-instruction (dual) time counted in full.
- Any PIC/US time counted in full.
- Any P2 time counted in full.
- Any student-pilot-in-command (SPIC) time counted in full up to a maximum of 50 hours toward the ATPL PIC time.
- Up to 100 hours in a helicopter flight simulator.
- Up to 30 hours in a touring motor glider (TMG) or glider.

Up to fifty per cent of each of the minimum experience amounts listed may be in fixed-wing aircraft.

The integrated course can start at *ab initio* level, and provides the qualification of a CPL(H) with Instrument Rating, Multi-Engine Rating and Multi-Crew Co-operation credit – a 'frozen ATPL'. It is aimed at training pilots to a level of proficiency to enable them to operate as co-pilot in multi-pilot, multi-engine helicopters in commercial air transportation. The course includes visual and instrument flying instruction, and multi-crew/multi-pilot helicopter training. It can last for a period of between twelve and thirty-six months. The flying training comprises a minimum of 195 hours, which must include the following:

- 125 hours of dual instruction.
- 70 hours as PIC, including at least 14 hours of solo day flying and 1 hour of solo night flying; 55 hours may be as student-pilot-in-command (SPIC).
- 50 hours of cross-country flying, including at least 10 hours as SPIC and a flight of at least 100 nautical miles with landings at two airfields other than the departure airfield.
- 5 hours of night flying, including 3 hours of dual instruction, 1 hour of solo cross-country flight, and five solo night circuits with five take-offs and landings.
- 50 hours of instrument time, of which 35 hours must be dual instruction (10 or 20 hours may be in a ground trainer of simulator, depending on type) and 15 hours must be as SPIC.
- 15 hours of multi-crew co-operation.

Holders of a PPL(H) may be credited with fifty per cent of the hours flown

Airline Transport Pilot Licence – Helicopters			
ATPL Approved Integrated Course Provides qualification of a CPL(H) with Instrument Rating and to co-pilot on multi-pilot, multi-engine helicopters in commercial air transportation 195hr flight training	125hr dual instruction (sub-section hours can form a combined function)	50hr instrument flying	35hr instrument flight instruction
			15hr SPIC
			15hr multi-crew operation for which a simulator may be used
		5hr night flying	Five solo circuits, including 5 take-offs and landings
			3hr dual instruction
			1hr night navigation
		55hr SPIC	
		14hr VFR flight as PIC	
		1hr night flight as PIC	
		50hr cross-country as PIC	Including a flight of at least 100 nautical miles that visits and lands at two different aerodromes
			At least 10hr as SPIC
Experience required: 1,000hr of flight time	350hr multi-pilot operation		
	250hr as PIC, or 100hr as PIC and 150hr as PIC/US		
	200hr cross-country	At least 70hr as PIC or PIC/US	
	70hr instrument flight time	No more than 30hr instrument ground time	
	100hr night flying as PIC, PIC/US or P2		

before starting the course, up to a maximum of 40 hours, of which no more than 20 hours may be dual instruction. If a night-flying qualification is held, the maximum credit rises to 50 hours, of which 25 hours may be dual instruction. All of the required training/experience hours must be flown before the final ATPL(H) Skill Test can be taken.

In addition, the integrated course includes 750 hours of theoretical-knowledge instruction for the ground examinations, all of which must be completed within the same continuous approved course. The fourteen papers cover the following subjects:

- Air Law.
- Aircraft General Knowledge (two papers).
- Flight Performance and Planning (three papers).
- Human Performance and Limitations.
- Meteorology.
- Navigation (two papers).
- Operational Procedures.
- Principles of Flight.
- Communications (two papers).

The pass mark is seventy-five per cent for each paper.

Applicants taking the modular route also require the theoretical-knowledge qualifications, and they must be attained by taking a modular Airline Transport Pilot Theoretical Knowledge Course at an approved training organization. A minimum qualification of a PPL(H) is required prior to taking the course, which involves 650 hours of instruction. The course must be completed within a period of eighteen months. A pass in the examinations is valid for seven years from the last validity date of the Instrument Rating issued for the ATPL, allowing time for the necessary flight experience to be gained prior to issue of the licence.

COMMERCIAL PILOT LICENCE COURSES

First, there is the most direct route – an approved, full-time integrated course leading to the issue of a 'frozen ATPL'. There are only a few approved flying schools in the UK that offer such courses on fixed-wing aircraft. As of January 2008, the CAA listed the following organizations: Cabair College of Air Training at Cranfield Aerodrome, CTC Aviation Training at Bournemouth Airport (also in New Zealand) and Oxford Aviation Training at Oxford Airport. The CAA lists are updated regularly, as required. (*See* Chapter 6 for contact details for these organizations.)

Ab initio ATPL courses last about thirteen months, and include full ground school, 40 hours of simulator training and a minimum of 200 hours of flying on single- and twin-engine light aircraft. The courses are full-time and (usually) residential. Normally, schools demand minimum educational

Because of the high cost of training, many commercial helicopter pilots come from the military. Their flying skills are in high demand, particularly for demanding jobs such as flying police helicopters and air ambulances, like this Eurocopter EC135.

standards of five passes at GCSE (or regional or national equivalent), to include English, mathematics and a science subject, preferably physics. These are school requirements and not official CAA policy, which lays down no educational standards, although most knowledgeable observers of professional pilot training say that *ab initio* students seeking professional licences should have A-level passes in mathematics and physics, otherwise they will find the ground school hard going.

It is wise, although not essential, to ensure that you meet the more stringent medical requirements for a JAR-FCL Class 1 medical certificate before embarking on a professional licence course. Although a Class 2 (PPL) medical certificate is adequate for the training period, a Class 1 certificate must be held before any commercial licence can be issued, and obviously it is pointless to pursue a training course, only to find at the end of it that you are debarred from obtaining your licence for medical reasons. The first medical examination for a professional licence must be conducted by a CAA Medical Branch examiner at Gatwick. Thereafter, the certificate can be renewed by a CAA-authorized medical examiner. The medical standards are higher than those for private pilots. For example, impaired hearing, which would not necessarily prevent a PPL applicant from obtaining a Class 2 medical certificate, would probably prohibit the issue of a professional certificate. Renewal intervals for Class 1 medical certificates are as follows:

- CPL holders in single-pilot air transport operations carrying passengers
  – annually up to forty years of age; six-monthly thereafter.
- CPL holders in other commercial operations – annually up to sixty
  years of age; six-monthly thereafter.
- ATPL holders – every six months.

How much does an ATPL course cost? At early-2008 prices, an approved full-time, integrated course would cost upwards of £60,000, inclusive of ground school, flying and VAT. Medical expenses, CAA examination and licence fees, any additional flying training needed beyond the minimum requirement and accommodation would add to that figure.

Not surprisingly, most of the self-financed students at commercial flying schools come from abroad. The traditional alternative to paying your own way (and incidentally having the money to pay does *not* guarantee a place on a course unless you meet the educational and aptitude requirements) was to find a sponsor which, in practice, meant an airline. By early 2008, such sponsorship schemes had become virtually non-existent, although that is not to say that sponsorship will never be available again – if pilots become in short supply in future, the major airlines may reintroduce their own cadet schemes. However, Oxford Aviation Training operates schemes with several airlines, whereby the airline covers part of the cost of a student's training and, subject to satisfactory completion of the course, the student pays back that cost by deductions from salary during the first few years of employment with the airline. Obviously, competition for such support is keen, and acceptance of a student is subject to a stringent assessment. Other schools run similar schemes with 'partner' airlines.

Various bursaries and scholarships are offered by a number of organizations to assist in flight training, and these are always worth pursuing. The British Air Line Pilots Association (BALPA) publishes a list of such sponsorships, while the Guild of Air Pilots and Air Navigators (GAPAN) also may be able to help in this respect (*see* Chapter 6 for contact details of these organizations). Alternatively, it may be possible to obtain a career development loan from a bank to cover some of the cost of a course. Such loans are designed so that you only begin to pay them back after you have completed the course and, hopefully, have found employment.

The larger training organizations often hold career-pilot seminars, which provide an insight into what is involved in training for a professional licence. Such seminars are well worth attending, as they give you the opportunity to gain useful information about the course, the training environment and the school's facilities. Such schools usually have contacts with airlines and may be able to help students find employment upon completion of the course.

A visit to a typical commercial pilot training establishment reveals just what an integrated ATPL course entails. Oxford Aviation Training, appropriately located within sight of the spires of the City of Oxford, that traditional seat of learning and scholarship, is one of the world's largest professional flight training establishments. Many of its students come from abroad, notably from the Middle East and Africa.

Oxford's integrated ATPL course lasts approximately sixty-eight weeks and begins with an initial fifteen-week period of intensive ground instruction. At the end of this period, students undergo a series of internal OAT tests in preparation for the first seven JAR exams. After a short break, there are another eleven weeks of ground school, followed by the remaining seven ATPL theoretical-knowledge exams. All fourteen exams must be passed before students move on to the Foundation Flight Training phase of the course, which takes place at Oxford's Airline Training Centre at Phoenix Goodyear Airport in Arizona, USA. There, the weather allows training to progress far more rapidly than it might in the UK.

This phase lasts twenty weeks and includes 105 hours of flight time on Piper Warrior aircraft, and 15 hours in an FNPT II simulator. Today, simulators play an invaluable part in professional flight training, particularly for instrument flight procedures. They save time and money, and, if used as an integral part of a well-planned training syllabus, permit more effective and economic use of aircraft for those parts of the syllabus that can best be taught in the air, such as take-offs and landings, recovery from unusual attitudes or visual cross-country flight. For instrument procedures, modern simulators can reproduce virtually everything that might be experienced in a real aircraft. Indeed, when converting pilots to new aircraft types in airline service, it is common for a trainee to get his or her first 'feel' of the real aircraft in the air quite late in the conversion course. Students also receive 15 hours of multi-engine training in the Piper PA-34 Seneca twin in Arizona. This is followed by the Multi-Engine CPL Skill Test and the issue of a CPL.

Students return to Oxford for the remainder of their training, which begins with an intensive two-week First Officer Fundamentals course. The purpose of this is to prepare new pilots for their intended role as first officers, or airline co-pilots, something that is not an essential step to a commercial licence, but that is of great benefit to anyone seeking an airline career. The course covers such subjects as first officer responsibilities, crew resource management, commercial appreciation and communication skills. In addition, this part of the course provides advice on job interview techniques and preparation of all-important CVs.

Next comes the Advanced Flight Training phase of the course, which comprises 50 hours of flying over an eleven-week period. This concentrates on multi-engine training, on the Seneca and simulators, and in poor weather and controlled airspace with airliner traffic. At the end of this phase, students take the Instrument Rating Skill Test to complete their CPL/IR.

The final part of the training is the 40-hour Multi-Crew and Jet Operations Course, which takes place over a period of three weeks. This is 'flown' in a Boeing 737-400 simulator, and teaches students how to work in a multi-crew environment and how to fly a modern jet airliner. On completion of this phase, students graduate from the course with a 'frozen

ATPL', and are ready to move on directly to an airline and airliner type-specific training.

While at Oxford and Phoenix, students live in comfortable motel-style study/bedrooms on the airfield. Unlike university undergraduates, they are required to wear the school's uniform during working hours, but otherwise the atmosphere is the comradely, cosmopolitan one of any university, although with longer working hours and perhaps a more purposeful air to the students, who are united by one common aim – to fly professionally, in both senses of the word.

Nonetheless, there is a drop-out rate of around twenty-five per cent among trainees. It sounds wasteful and disappointing for students to work so hard and fail to obtain their licences, but most of the failures occur very early in the course, usually within the first three months, and before the students make their first solo flights. This is because the integrated ATPL course is intensive from the outset, and failure to cope either in the classroom or in the air quickly manifests itself. Moreover, the time allocated for the course is not too generous, so there is seldom an opportunity for a student who falls seriously behind to catch up.

Training Concessions for Experienced Pilots

The CAA grants certain exemptions from the training requirements for military pilots and for licensed private pilots taking the approved CPL and CPL/IR courses. Pilots qualified and serving with the UK's armed forces, and who are in current military flying practice with total hours exceeding the minimum licence requirements for the CPL, can count their military flight time toward a professional licence. The approved professional flying schools offer ground and flying courses specially tailored to ex-military personnel attempting to gain civilian commercial licences. Private pilots may be granted a partial exemption from the minimum number of training hours laid down for approved CPL and CPL/IR courses at the discretion of the flying training organization. However, because of the integrated nature of these CPL courses, combining alternating ground and flight elements, such an exemption will probably not reduce the total duration of the course, although it can reduce the overall cost by the number of flying hours credited for PPL experience.

The Modular Route

For would-be professional pilots who cannot finance an integrated course in one go, or who do not want to commit to a full-time course, the modular route to a CPL/IR allows them to gain the qualifications and necessary experience on a step-by-step basis. Such a course still represents a substantial financial outlay, although the total would be significantly less (perhaps a little more than half) than the cost of an integrated course. On the other hand, since completing the training is likely to take several years, there is the risk that the cost of modules may rise with the passage of time. However, undertaking a modular course does allow the individual to continue in at least part-time employment and possibly live at home while completing the training, providing a useful saving.

A typical *ab initio* modular course would be broken down into the following stages:

1. Private Pilot Licence, Night Qualification, IMC Rating, Multi-Engine Rating.
2. Theoretical-Knowledge examinations (ATPL).
3. Commercial Pilot Licence.
4. Instrument Rating.
5. Multi-Crew Co-operation Course.

Subject to satisfactory passes of the theoretical-knowledge examinations and Skill Test, this would lead to a 'frozen ATPL'.

Under the modular system, the theoretical-knowledge training can be undertaken on a full-time course, which can last for twenty-seven weeks, or by distance learning over a period of a year.

Most students on a modular course are likely to be aiming for an ATPL, and therefore will choose to train for an Instrument Rating after gaining the CPL. However, a CPL is also needed by anyone who wants to become a flying instructor and who wants to be paid for instructing (with the correct rating, you can instruct unpaid as the holder of a PPL). Consequently, at Stage 4, some may opt to train for a Flight Instructor Rating instead of for an IR.

THE FLIGHT INSTRUCTOR RATING

In the past, flying instruction was used by many aspiring professional pilots as a means of hours building on the way to a commercial licence. Prior to the adoption of the JAR-FCL rules, the CAA offered substantial reductions in the training requirements for a CPL to those who had amassed a large amount of flight time. The trick was to find a way of gaining that time as cheaply as possible (one way was to buy an aircraft, or a share in one, which could be sold when the hours had been gained). The best way was a job that provided lots of flying and a salary, and that was instructing. Known as the self-improver route, this produced significant savings in the cost of training. In those days, to be paid for instructing, all one needed was a PPL with an Assistant Flying Instructor Rating or a Flying Instructor Rating. Subsequently, the rules were changed and it became necessary to obtain a Basic Commercial Pilot Licence (BCPL) in addition to the PPL, although the training/experience requirements for this were far less exacting than for a full CPL. Today, however, it is no longer possible to be paid for instructing unless the instructor holds a CPL, and the Assistant Flying Instructor Rating no longer exists. Instead, there is a Flight Instructor Rating, which carries a

Flight Instructor – Aeroplanes – to instruct to PPL(A) level		
Experience: 200hr flight time	100hr as PIC if holding a CPL(A) or 150hr as PIC if holding a PPL(A)	
	At least 30hr in single-engine piston aircraft	5hr must have been completed during the six months preceding the pre-entry flight test
	10hr instrument flight	Not more than 5hr in a flight trainer or simulator
	20hr cross-country as PIC	Including a cross-country flight of at least 300 nautical miles, landing at two different aerodromes
FI approved course 30hr flight instruction	25hr must be dual flight instruction	5hr may be 'mutual flying' (with another FI applicant)
	5hr may be in an approved flight trainer or simulator	
	The skill test is additional to the training time	

'Restricted' endorsement until the holder has gained some experience of instructing. There are also several specialized instructor ratings, such as Instrument Rating Instructor, Class Rating Instructor, Type Rating Instructor and Synthetic Flight Instructor (for carrying out training on ground-based simulators).

As with other licences and ratings, it is necessary to undertake an approved course of training to obtain a JAR-FCL Flight Instructor Rating (FI). Prior to taking the course, however, the aspiring instructor must meet certain minimum requirements and undergo a pre-entry flight test to assess his or her ability to complete the course. For an FI (Aeroplanes), these include a minimum age of eighteen and holding either a PPL or CPL, the latter if paid work will be sought, with an SEP Rating. A PPL holder must have completed at least 200 hours of flight time, of which 150 hours must be as pilot-in-command. In addition, regardless of licence held, the candidate must have logged the following: 30 hours of single-engine piston-aircraft time, of which at least 5 hours must have been flown within the six months preceding the pre-entry flight test; at least 10 hours of instrument flight instruction (up to 5 hours in a ground trainer or simulator); and 20 hours of cross-country flying (including a flight of 300 nautical miles with landings at two separate airfields other than the departure airfield).

The course itself comprises a minimum of 30 hours of flight training, of which 25 hours must be dual instruction (5 hours may be in a ground trainer or simulator). The remaining 5 hours may be flown with another FI applicant. In addition, there are 125 hours of theoretical-knowledge training, comprising 40 hours of tuition, 78 hours of teaching practice and 7 hours of progress tests. A candidate who holds a PPL must also meet the knowledge requirements for the grant of a CPL.

The rating will be issued upon completion of a Skill Test with an authorized examiner. During this, the candidate is required to demonstrate the ability to instruct student pilots to the level required for the grant of a PPL(A). As mentioned, the FI Rating will have a 'Restricted' endorsement at first, and the holder can only practise the privileges of the rating under the supervision of a fully qualified and authorized FI. In addition, the holder of a Restricted FI cannot give approval for a student to undertake his or her first solo day or night flight, or first solo cross-country navigation flight.

For the restriction to be removed, the holder of the Restricted FI needs to have completed at least 100 hours of flight instruction, to have supervised at least twenty-five student solo flights, and to have received a recommendation for the restriction to be removed from the supervising FI. On completion of 500 hours total flying time, the options are then available via various approved courses to extend the rating to instruct for the CPL, single-pilot-multi-engine and class ratings, and PPL FI Rating. For each of these ratings, the instructor needs to hold the rating that will be taught. For instance, a CPL instructor needs to hold a CPL.

In the long term, with 200 hours of instrument flying under your belt, the qualification can be extended to instruct pilots to IR standard. The ratings do not end there; after all, someone has to instruct multi-engine, multi-pilot instructors, but as that requires 1,500 hours on multi-pilot aircraft and a few other requisites, this book will restrict itself to the basic FI rating.

Helicopters

The minimum age for an unrestricted FI (Helicopters) rating is eighteen years. Before candidates can start training, they must have logged at least 250 hours of flight time, of which 100 hours must be as PIC if holding an ATPL(H) or CPL(H), or 200 hours as PIC if holding a PPL(H). Ten hours of instrument flight instruction must have been received, of which 5 hours may be instrument ground time in a flight simulator or trainer. At least 20 hours of cross-country flight as PIC must have been logged, including a flight of not less than 100 nautical miles during which two full-stop landings at two different aerodromes must have been made. A specific pre-entry flight test is also required to be passed within the six months preceding the start of the training course, and an approved course of theoretical-knowledge instruction must also have been passed. The flight training comprises at least 30 hours of instruction, including 25 hours dual. The remaining 5 hours can be 'mutual flying' (two FI trainees flying together). As with fixed-wing

Flight Instructor – Helicopters		
Minimum 250hr flight time plus 30hr flight instruction	200hr PIC if a PPL(H) holder or 100hr PIC if an ATPL(H) or CPL(H) holder	
	10hr instrument instruction	5hr may be instrument ground time
	20hr cross-country as PIC	Including a flight of at least 100 nautical miles that visits and lands at two different aerodromes
	25hr dual instruction	
	5hr may be 'mutual flying'	

aircraft, initially the rating is issued on a restricted basis, the same restrictions applying. This restriction can be lifted after the instructor has completed at least 100 hours of flight instruction, supervised twenty-five student solo flights and received a recommendation from the supervising FI. Although then classed as unrestricted, the rating does not allow the instructor to carry out all types of flight instruction until at least 500 hours of flight time in helicopters have been logged.

Because of the high cost of helicopter operations, from a financial point of view, a full CPL and FI rating is best reserved for helicopter-mad National Lottery winners, unless exemption from training has been gained through UK military forces training.

Funding

Some large flying schools may offer sponsorship schemes whereby some or all of the FI course fees are paid in return for a period of instructing on the staff of the school. The Cabair Group, based at Cranfield Aerodrome, and Oxford Aviation are among those that have provided such sponsored training in the past. It is worth asking the school you trained with to see if this is a possibility. In addition, the Guild of Air Pilots and Air Navigators sometimes offers FI scholarships, while the British Air Line Pilots Association publishes details of a variety of bursaries and sponsorship schemes on its web site, some of which cover FI costs. You will probably still have to cover the cost of a CPL if you want remuneration for your instructing.

Another possible source of finance for FI courses is a career-development loan from a bank, which will not have to be repaid until a while after the course, by which time you should be in employment.

Bear in mind that not everyone is temperamentally suited to becoming an instructor, and the financial rewards are small. The most common complaint of flying instructors the world over is that they are overworked and underpaid. That said, it is a good means of remaining in current flying practice, amassing some hours and earning some money for those who have gained a professional licence, but have yet to find an airline job.

TRAINING ABROAD

Another option worth considering for obtaining a CPL is to go overseas to obtain your training. You may have seen in aviation magazines tempting advertisements from American flight schools that offer 'Commercial and Instrument Tickets in Sunny Florida in Only 90 Days!' These usually quote amazingly low prices which, allowing extra for return transatlantic air fares and accommodation, still come out substantially below the cost of a British CPL/IR course. There has to be a snag – and there is. A US FAA CPL is not valid for the commercial operation of a British registered aircraft. In other words, it does not entitle you to earn a living by flying British aircraft in Britain. Unlike the private licence, which can usually be validated locally in foreign countries without too much fuss, there is no reciprocal arrangement whereby an American (or any other non-JAA state) commercial licence can be converted readily to a JAR-FCL CPL.

That is not to say that an American CPL cannot be converted to a JAR-FCL CPL at all. It can be done, but at a cost. For a start, the applicant must meet the experience requirements of the JAR licence and must hold a Class 1 medical certificate. Sufficient ground training must be undertaken to pass all of the JAR-FCL CPL theoretical-knowledge examinations. If the candidate wants to take the JAR-FCL ATPL theoretical-knowledge exams, then he or she must undertake the entire 650-hour ground-school course for those examinations and pass them at the end of the course. A certain amount of flying training will also be necessary, again as determined by an approved training provider, but to include at least five hours on a complex aircraft type if this has not been done already. At the end of this training, it is necessary to pass the CPL Skill Test. A UK Flight Radiotelephony Operator's Licence will be required as well. A non-JAR-FCL Instrument Rating can be converted in a similar manner, following further theoretical-knowledge and flight training, together with passes of the relevant examinations and Skill Test.

So, obtaining an American qualification is no shortcut, and clearly it is likely to be much more expensive than at first it might appear. Do not believe any claim that a course offered by a US flight school guarantees exemption from British requirements (or a job!) when you get back home. However, if you gain a US commercial licence and use it to build flying hours cheaply in the USA, where aircraft hire rates are much lower than those in Britain, the hours logged (or at least a proportion of them) could be counted toward the minima for a JAR-FCL CPL.

That said, there are a number of overseas training establishments that offer instruction for JAR-FCL private and commercial licences. These have the advantage of lower operating costs than in the UK, leading to substantial reductions in the total cost of training. Moreover, they are usually in areas that benefit from better weather, allowing training to progress at a relatively rapid rate. They operate to the same syllabus as UK schools, employing JAR-FCL qualified instructors and examiners. Naturally, care should be taken when committing to a course of training overseas and, ideally, establishments should be visited prior to enrolling. Be wary of outlandish claims. Remember the old adage: 'If it sounds too good to be true, it probably is'.

THE JOB MARKET

What kind of employment can a newly qualified professional pilot expect to be offered? It would be unwise to think of the licence itself as the key to a wide choice of flying jobs. A freshly issued licence, with all of 150 or 200 hours logged, is unlikely to bring prospective employers beating a path to your door. A CPL without an IR is *very* limiting, as a CPL/IR is mandatory for the commander or co-pilot of any aircraft engaged in scheduled or charter public transport services. A non-IR commercial pilot would be restricted to a narrow choice of activities such as instructing, pleasure flying, perhaps aerial photography of a non-specialized nature, acting as co-pilot on an aircraft not legally required to have two crew members, or agricultural aviation. However, agricultural flying is an extremely specialized and skilled business, and few operators will hire pilots with fewer than 500 hours of experience in the work.

This 'must have experience' requirement is a common stumbling block for the newly qualified CPL. How can you gain experience without a flying job, for which you need experience? The answer, most frequently, is to swallow your pride, pocket your bright new CPL and accept employment in some lesser capacity than first pilot to gain access to experience building opportunities. In this respect, a pilot who can offer some other skills outside the cockpit, such as engineer, salesman, accountant, office clerk or even van driver, might stand a better chance of attracting an employer than one who can fly, full stop.

The CPL/IR holder is in a stronger position, because under JAR rules, this licence/rating permits the holder to act as captain of light aircraft and to act as co-pilot in any aircraft certificated for two crew not involved in public transport, also as co-pilot in public-transport aircraft below 5,700kg, such as the Beechcraft King Air and Embraer Bandeirante. To captain an airliner in commercial service, an ATPL is necessary.

Setting aside airline employment, the opportunities for CPL/IRs in general aviation are varied, and air-taxi work is an obvious possibility. Most air-taxi operators will require captains to have logged a minimum of 1,000 hours flying time, of which 500 hours must be as pilot-in-command, but co-pilot positions are available to those with less experience. A fixed-base operation, which offers flying instruction and *ad hoc* charter work, would also be a good, although not highly-paid, starting point for a new CPL willing to instruct and undertake commercial charter flying. Similar openings occur from time to time with operators of private business aircraft.

What are the chances of a newly qualified commercial pilot getting an airline job? Naturally, it depends on the state of the job market at the time, but in recent years, the growth in regional air services and 'third-level' carriers, often operating relatively unsophisticated twin-turboprop aircraft, has increased both the opportunities for employment and the demand for commercial pilot training courses.

Apart from a mandatory CPL/IR, the minimum experience level which any airline will normally set before considering a pilot is 1,000 hours. As a rule, pilots are selected on the assumption that they may become captains. The days when airline captains were aloof from the remainder of the crew are long gone. Now, more than ever, they are a part of a team, and airlines look for people who can get along with their colleagues, on the flight deck and in the cabin, and with the passengers. These are the people who will be sufficiently self-confident and assertive not to hesitate to question an action on the flight deck if the need arises. In essence, airline captains are high achievers, strong, socially confident leaders, possessing team skills and an awareness of the business needs of the airline.

A common thread that runs through every success story of pilots attaining airline positions is dedication to achieving that goal. There are no guarantees, no shortcuts. The route is long, arduous, expensive in time and money, and often dispiriting, but for those who make it (and it has to be said that many do not), ultimately it is very rewarding. For a greater insight into what is involved in training for the flight deck of an airliner, refer to Andrew Cook's informative book, *To Be an Airline Pilot* (Airlife).

The commercial pilot job market is cyclical, and in a book of this kind, it is clearly impossible to predict just where employment openings might occur at any future time, but besides the obvious source of vacancies advertised in the aviation press, trade organizations such as the Aircraft Owners and Pilots Association, the British Air Line Pilots Association, the British Business and General Aviation Association, the British Helicopter Advisory Board, and the Guild of Air Pilots and Air Navigators can probably offer advice on the current situation.

CHAPTER 5
THE MILITARY
PILOT

A career with the armed services offers some of the finest pilot training and certainly the most exciting flying in the world. Consequently, competition for a trainee pilot's position is extremely fierce and the selection procedures are rigorous, and with good cause, for the cost of training a Royal Air Force fast-jet pilot to squadron service standard runs into millions of pounds. Small wonder, then, that for every 200 enquiries received from aspiring service pilots, on average only one will successfully negotiate the selection and training procedures to become an RAF pilot.

THE ROYAL AIR FORCE

The RAF recruits aircrew officers either directly (from school, university or civilian life) or via an RAF sponsored university cadetship scheme. A major change in recruitment policy was announced twenty years ago, following a study that recommended broadening the opportunities for women in the service. They became eligible to serve as pilots and navigators for the first time since the formation of the RAF in 1918. Today, women pilots are permitted to fly fast jets, combat helicopters, transports, tankers, airborne-early-warning and search-and-rescue aircraft, and to serve as flying instructors.

The minimum age and educational requirements for RAF aircrew entrants are as follows. School-leavers, graduates and civilians must be aged between 17½ and 24 years on entry, although application must be made before reaching the age of 23½. They must have at least two passes at A Level plus five GCSEs (or equivalent) at Grade C or above, including English language and mathematics. Applicants must be subjects or citizens of Great Britain or the Republic of Ireland, or must have been born in a country that is (or was) within the British Commonwealth or Republic of Ireland, or have both parents who meet (or met) those qualifications. In exceptional circumstances, a dispensation against these requirements may be made at the discretion of the Secretary of State for Defence, but all applicants must possess British nationality at the time of application, and applicants not of UK origin must normally have been resident in the UK for a minimum period of five years.

After basic training on the Short Tucano, RAF and RN fast-jet pilots transition on to the BAE Hawk for their first taste of jet flying. (Adrian Pingstone)

As part of the RAF's Graduate Entry Scheme, sponsorships are available to undergraduates and prospective undergraduates taking full-time degree courses at a recognized UK educational establishment.

University Air Squadrons

Before examining the Royal Air Force's selection and training procedures, it is worth looking at the role played by the University Air Squadrons (UASs). Lord Trenchard conceived the idea of forming Air Squadrons at the Oxford and Cambridge Universities in 1919, with the declared object of 'encouraging an interest in flying, and promoting and maintaining liaison with universities in technical and research problems affecting aviation … [and] to assist those who wished to take up aeronautics as a profession, either in the Royal Air Force or in a civilian capacity, and those who, while not making aviation their career, desired to give part-time service to defence in the non-regular air force.'

That is precisely the function of the fourteen UASs that exist today under direct command of the Director Elementary Flying Training Headquarters, University and Air Cadets, at the RAF College at Cranwell in Lincolnshire. The UASs make up the largest flying training organization within the RAF, and are affiliated to about eighty universities and university colleges throughout the British Isles. They provide approximately sixty per cent of the RAF's new pilots.

There are three classes of University Air Squadron membership: RAF Volunteer Reserve members, University Bursars and University Cadets. RAF

Volunteer Reservists are undergraduates who want to learn to fly, but initially are under no obligation to join the RAF. Recruitment is usually carried out within the first week of a new university year, and applications exceed available places by a factor of four or five to one. RAF(VR) members are enlisted as Airmen or Airwomen, but enjoy the status of Officer Cadets. While they do not have to undergo the rigorous aptitude tests that RAF aircrew entrants must take, RAF(VR) members must pass medical and selection boards before being allowed to fly service aircraft. RAF(VR) membership of UASs is normally limited to two years, but may be extended for a further year to those seriously interested in pursuing an RAF career.

University Bursar and University Cadet UAS members are sponsored by the RAF following acceptance by the Department of Officer Recruitment and selection at the RAF College, Cranwell. University Bursars are committed to Short Service Commissions with the RAF after university graduation. University Cadets are commissioned and paid as acting pilot officers while studying, and after graduation enter the service as junior officers. As of early 2008, however, University Cadetship was restricted to medical students only. All RAF-sponsored undergraduates, including those destined for careers in the ground branches of the service, automatically become UAS members.

In a typical UAS, RAF(VR) members outnumber University Bursars and University Cadets by more than two to one. Individual squadron membership varies between forty and eighty, according to the number and size of educational establishments served. The geographic spread of UASs is such that few major educational centres are denied access to a squadron within an acceptable travelling distance.

The UAS pilot training course provides for 10–15 hours of flying per year, although it may be possible to increase this by taking up the unused training allocation of other UAS members who choose not to fly. For RAF(VR) members, this training can be used toward a civilian NPPL after taking any necessary extra tuition together with the relevant CAA examinations and flight tests. However, this is not an aim of UAS membership, and the credit of hours toward a civilian licence is at the discretion of the CAA.

UAS flying courses are conducted on a fleet of ninety Grob 115E Tutor two-seat trainers. The training syllabus comprises general handling and circuit procedures leading to first solo (usually after eleven hours of dual instruction), instrument training and navigation. Students' progress is closely monitored and tested at 'critical points', each of which must be passed satisfactorily before moving on to the next stage of training.

The UASs provide an excellent opportunity for young people to experience flying in a service environment. Military discipline has to be observed and uniform worn, and a substantial commitment of time is demanded, typically one or two half-days each week during term time for flying training, and one evening per week for ground studies. However, care is taken to ensure that over-enthusiastic pilots do not neglect their academic studies in favour of flying! During the university summer vacations, UASs deploy to RAF stations for a four-week summer camp devoted to concentrated flying and gaining an insight into service life. In addition, there is a wide range of sporting and social activities, and inter-squadron competitions to be enjoyed.

As of early 2008, the following University Air Squadrons were active:

UAS	Academic institutions served	Base
Birmingham	Aston University Birmingham University Coventry University Keele University Staffordshire University University of Wolverhampton University of Central England in Birmingham Warwick University	RAF Cosford
Bristol	Bath University Bristol University Exeter University Plymouth University University of the West of England at Bristol	RAF Colerne
Cambridge	Anglia Polytechnic Cambridge University University of East Anglia University of Essex	RAF Wyton
East Midlands	Leicester De Montfort University Nottingham University Leicester University Loughborough University Nottingham Trent University	RAF Cranwell
East of Scotland	Aberdeen University Dundee University Robert Gordon University St Andrews University University of Abertay, Dundee Edinburgh University Heriot-Watt University Napier University Stirling University	RAF Leuchars

Glasgow and Strathclyde	Glasgow University Glasgow Caledonian University Strathclyde University University of Paisley	Glasgow Airport
Liverpool	Lancaster University Liverpool University Liverpool John Moores University University of Central Lancashire	RAF Woodvale
University of London	Brunel University Canterbury College, Kent City University Greenwich University Hertfordshire University Kingston University London University University of Kent	RAF Wyton

Manchester and Salford	Manchester University
	Salford University
	University of Manchester Institute
	  of Science & Technology
	Manchester Metropolitan
	  University
		RAF Woodvale

Northumbrian	Durham University Newcastle University University of Northumbria at Newcastle University of Sunderland University of Teeside	RAF Leeming
Oxford	Oxford Brookes University Oxford University Reading University	RAF Benson
Southampton	Southampton University University of Portsmouth	RAF Boscombe Down

University of Wales	St David's University College,
	  Lampeter
	University College of Wales,
	  Aberystwyth
	University of Glamorgan
		RAF St Athan

University of Wales College of
  Cardiff
University College of North Wales
University College of Swansea
University of Wales College of
  Medicine

Yorkshire	Bradford University	RAF Church
	Hull University	Fenton
	Leeds Metropolitan University	
	Leeds University	
	Sheffield Hallam University	
	Sheffield University	
	University of Huddersfield	
	University of Humberside	
	York University	

For details of individual UASs, contact the individual university direct, or visit the UAS web site: www.universityairsquadrons.com. Alternatively, write to: The Officer Commanding, University Air Squadrons, RAF Cranwell, Sleaford, Lincolnshire NG34 8HB.

Selecting Aircrew for the Royal Air Force

Direct Entrants and university-sponsored entrants begin their RAF careers with an application to the Officer and Aircrew Selection Centre (OASC) at RAF College Cranwell. Application is made on a six-part form, which has sections for personal, educational, previous employment, recreation, previous military service, flying experience and general information.

The selection of potential aircrew is carried out by The Air Board, and the four-part selection process at Cranwell takes four days. Applicants arrive at Cranwell on a Sunday for briefings and orientation. On the second day, candidates take aptitude tests aimed at finding out how each will respond to aircrew training, measuring their ability to learn rather than their ability to perform at this stage.

The OASC uses computer-based aptitude tests for prospective aircrew. Applicants for all the British services and some overseas forces are tested, with an annual throughput of 8,000 potential pilots, navigators and controllers.

The computer equipment analyses a candidate's co-ordination of hand, eye and foot; rate control; instrument interpretation; spatial awareness; memory; deductive reasoning; selective attention; information scheduling; and perceptual speed. All of these are valuable pointers to a candidate's ability to fly, navigate and fight in a modern jet aircraft. These tests can take up to six hours.

On the third day of the selection process, candidates undergo a thorough medical examination and a character-assessment interview. Those candidates

An RAF Tornado GR4 in action during Operation *Iraqi Freedom*. A multi-role aircraft, the Tornado is the RAF's primary strike aircraft, and a large number are retained. However, the F3 variants are to be replaced by the Typhoon. (US Dept of Defense)

who have passed the aptitude tests and the medical, and who show promise at the interview are selected to take part in 'syndicate tests'. Each 'syndicate' consists of a team of five or six candidates, who are supplied with numbered overalls to preserve their anonymity. The syndicate is boarded by two officers who assess each candidate through five different exercises: Practical Team, Discussion, Planning (Theoretical), an Individual Theoretical Problem and Individually Led Practical. The idea is that the subsequent conversations will reveal how each applicant responds to others, whether he or she mixes easily or is reticent, and whether he or she is a natural leader or a follower. The syndicate is presented with a planning exercise in which a specific task is outlined, and the candidates must draw up a plan of action and justify their decisions. The final round of team tests consists of a practical exercise (for example, crossing a hangar floor without touching the ground, using only a couple of planks and some suspended motor tyres), which has all the appearance of a practice session for the Royal Tournament. This is aimed at assessing qualities of leadership, courage, judgement, enthusiasm, initiative and determination.

Those who complete the selection course satisfactorily can usually expect to hear whether they have been accepted for aircrew entry or a university cadetship within a month of their visit to the OASC. Rejected applicants may re-apply for further assessment at the OASC provided they have not exceeded the maximum age limits for entry. At least twelve months must elapse before subsequent re-application. Those who fail the flying aptitude tests may be invited to consider non-aircrew careers if they have opted for alternatives on their initial applications.

Aircrew Training

Having been selected, new aircrew recruits for the RAF undergo a thirty-week Initial Officer Training course at the RAF College at Cranwell in Lincolnshire. The IOT course prepares entrants for their responsibilities as junior RAF officers. It includes drill routine, assault courses, initiative tests, survival training and general physical activities, such as canoeing and mountain climbing.

After IOT, all recruits receive ground-school training at RAF Cranwell. Direct entrants with no previous flying experience undergo sixty-two hours of elementary flying training in Grob 115E Tutor training aircraft at one of the fourteen University Air Squadrons. On completion of the Elementary Flying Training (EFT) course, pilots are required to pass a Final Handling Test, after which they are 'streamed' for the type of operational aircraft for which they are considered best suited: fast jet, multi-engine or helicopters. Most newly trained pilots are streamed for fast jets, since this is the RAF's primary operational requirement.

Pilots selected for fast jets progress to Basic Fast-Jet Training on the Tucano at RAF Linton-on-Ouse, where they complete a 120-hour course. On completion of the course, pilots are posted to No. 4 FTS at RAF Valley, where they are taught advanced flying, tactics and weapons training on the BAE Hawk T1. Twenty pilots each year are sent to complete their tactical weapons training on the Hawk 115 as part of the NATO Flying Training in Canada programme. At the end of these courses, pilots are assessed for either single- or two-seat operations, and most progress to an Operational Conversion Unit (OCU) to train on the actual type of front-line aircraft they will fly with a squadron, such as the Harrier, Tornado or Typhoon.

In time of crisis, the OCUs would play an active role, either as reinforcements for other squadrons operating the same type of aircraft, or by assuming squadron status, to which end some have 'reserve squadron' status.

Pilots selected for multi-engine training undergo a 30-hour Multi-Engine Lead-In course on the Slingsby Firefly before transferring to 45 (R) Squadron at RAF Cranwell for a 30-, 40- or 70-hour Advanced Flying Training course on the Beechcraft 200. On completion of the AFT course, they progress to an OCU for conversion training before being posted to an operational squadron.

Those pilots chosen for helicopter training go straight to the Defence Helicopter Flying School at RAF Shawbury to complete a 36-hour basic training course, followed by 37 hours of advanced training, in both cases on the Squirrel HT1. Then they carry out 65 hours of multi-engine flying on the Griffin HT1 before going on to complete 15 hours of search-and-rescue (SAR) training. After that, they are posted to an OCU followed by a front-line squadron.

The complete RAF training pattern is illustrated by the following list:

RAF Training and Operational Conversion Units

Unit	Aircraft type(s)	Station
Joint Elementary Flying Training School	Firefly M260/M260A	RAF Barkston Heath
No 1 FTS 72 (R) Sqn 207 (R) Sqn	Tucano	RAF Linton-on-Ouse
No 3 FTS 45 (R) Sqn 55 (R) Sqn	King Air B200, Dominie T1/T2, Tutor T1	RAF Cranwell
No 4 FTS 19 (R) Sqn 208 (R) Sqn	Hawk T1/T1A	RAF Valley
Defence Helicopter Flying School 60 (R) Sqn CFS	Squirrel HT1, Griffin HT1	RAF Shawbury
Search and Rescue Training Flight	Griffin HT1	RAF Valley
OCUs 15 (R) Sqn	Tornado GR4	RAF Lossiemouth
17 (R) Sqn	Typhoon	RAF Coningsby
29 (R) Sqn	Typhoon	RAF Coningsby
42 (R) Sqn	Nimrod MR2	RAF Kinloss
56 (R) Sqn	Tornado F3	RAF Leuchars
203 (R) Sqn	Sea King HAR3	RAF St Mawgan
Fast Jet and Weapons Operational Evaluation Unit	Tornado F3/GR4	RAF Coningsby

(R) indicates training unit/reserve squadron. These squadrons have a mobilization role.

Eventually scheduled to equip seven squadrons, the Eurofighter Typhoon is the RAF's latest fast-jet type. Tasked with air defence and ground attack, it can carry up to six medium-range and two short-range air-to-air missiles, as well as a variety of air-to-ground weapons. (Adrian Pingstone)

Direct Entrant aircrew recruits assume the rank of Aircraftman or Aircraftwoman (Officer Cadet) on entering the RAF and are commissioned after completing the IOT course, while sponsored graduates are commissioned as Pilot Officers on entry. There are two types of RAF commission. A Permanent Commission, subject to satisfactory completion of all training phases, is to the age of fifty-five, with an optional retirement date at the earliest age of thirty-eight or after completion of sixteen years of commissioned service, whichever comes later. It carries a pension, which is index-linked from the age of fifty-five. Short Service Commissions, which are not overly emphasized by the RAF for pilot entrants because of the high cost of training, are for twelve years, with an option to leave with a tax-free gratuity after eight years.

Promotion to Flying Officer and thence to Flight Lieutenant is automatic. A graduate entrant will typically reach the rank of Flight Lieutenant within two years of entry, and could be considered for promotion to the rank of Squadron Leader after his or her first tour of squadron duty, although such a promotion would not be likely to be granted immediately. A Direct Entrant takes about six years to achieve the rank of Flight Lieutenant. Promotion beyond that rank is subject to written examinations, with promotions decided on the merit of annual performance reports from squadron commanders.

Promotion to the rank of Squadron Leader and beyond can only be offered to holders of Permanent Commissions. There is also a Reserve Service requirement of four years additional service in the event of recall

The Boeing Chinook is the RAF's heavy-lift helicopter, capable of delivering large numbers of troops and their equipment to the battlefield. (Adrian Pingstone)

during a national emergency. The Permanent Commission carries a pension and a tax-free gratuity equal to three times the annual pension after sixteen years of service. The RAF promotion ladder looks like this:

Pilot Officer
Flying Officer
Flight Lieutenant
Squadron Leader
Wing Commander
Group Captain
Air Commodore
Air Vice-Marshal
Air Marshal
Air Chief Marshal
Marshal of the RAF

Squadron Service

At the end of operational conversion, the newly trained RAF pilot is given his or her first appointment (known as a 'posting') to an operational RAF squadron, which is the service's basic working unit. Pilots do get an opportunity to state a preference for a particular posting, but there is no guarantee that personal wishes can be accommodated. Tours of duty (the period between postings) usually last about thirty months.

To give some idea of the scope of the RAF in the early twenty-first century, and the geographical spread of operational squadrons within RAF Strike Command, the following list provides details of squadrons, the aircraft they operate and their regular bases. Strike Command is responsible for strike/attack and offensive support, air defence, reconnaissance, maritime patrol and anti-submarine attack, search and rescue, transport, aerial refuelling and helicopter operations.

Squadron	Aircraft Type(s)	Station
No. 1	Harrier GR9/9A	RAF Cottesmore
No. 2	Tornado GR4A	RAF Marham
No. 3	Typhoon	RAF Coningsby
No. 4	Harrier GR7/7A	RAF Cottesmore
No. 5	Sentinel R1	RAF Waddington
No. 7	Chinook HC2	RAF Odiham
No. 8	Sentry AEW1	RAF Waddington
No. 9	Tornado GR4	RAF Marham
No. 12	Tornado GR4	RAF Lossiemouth
No. 13	Tornado GR4A	RAF Marham
No. 14	Tornado GR4	RAF Lossiemouth
No. 18	Chinook HC2	RAF Odiham
No. 22	Sea King HAR3/3A	RMB Chivenor and detachments
No. 23	Sentry AEW	RAF Waddington
No. 24	Hercules C3/C4/C5	RAF Lyneham
No. 25	Tornado F3	RAF Leeming
No. 27	Chinook HC2	RAF Odiham
No. 28	Merlin HC3	RAF Benson
No. 30	Hercules C3/C4/C5	RAF Lyneham
No. 31	Tornado GR4	RAF Marham
No. 32	BAE 125 CC3, BAE 146 CC2 Agusta A109	RAF Northolt
No. 33	Puma HC1	RAF Benson
No. 39	Canberra PR9	RAF Marham
No. 43	Tornado F3	RAF Leuchars
No. 47	Hercules C1/C3/C4/C5	RAF Lyneham
No. 51	Nimrod R1	RAF Waddington
No. 70	Hercules C1/C3/C4/C5	RAF Lyneham
No. 78	Chinook HC2 Sea King HAR3/3A	RAF Mount Pleasant (Falkland Islands)
No. 84	Griffin HR2	RAF Akrotiri (Cyprus)
No. 99	C-17 Globemaster	RAF Brize Norton
No. 100	Hawk T1/T1A	RAF Leeming
No. 101	VC10 K3/K4/C1K	RAF Brize Norton
No. 111	Tornado F3	RAF Leuchars
No. 120	Nimrod MR2	RAF Kinloss

No. 201	Nimrod MR2	RAF Kinloss
No. 202	Sea King HAR3/3A	RAF Boulmer and detachments
No. 216	TriStar K1/KC1/C2/C2A	RAF Brize Norton
No. 230	Puma HC1	RAF Aldergrove
No. 617	Tornado GR4	RAF Lossiemouth
1312 Flight	Hercules C1	RAF Mount Pleasant
	VC10 K3/4	
1435 Flight	Tornado F3	RAF Mount Pleasant

The Air Training Corps

The Air Training Corps (ATC) was formed in 1941 to provide pre-entry training for boys planning careers in the RAF or Fleet Air Arm (FAA). After the war, the ATC was remodelled and its scope expanded. Its present-day function is as a national voluntary youth organization open to both boys and girls. It exists to encourage a practical interest in aviation, adventure and sport that will be useful in both service and civilian life.

The age limits for joining the ATC are thirteen to eighteen years, although cadets can remain in the corps until they reach the age of twenty, after which many become staff or instructors within the corps. The establishment of the ATC is for a maximum of 40,000 cadets supervised by up to 9,000 adult staff, administered from Headquarters Air Cadets at RAF Cranwell at Sleaford in Lincolnshire. There are six ATC regions:

- Central & East
- London & South East
- North
- Scotland & Northern Ireland
- South West
- Wales & West

These administer thirty-six Wings, and approximately 1,000 Squadrons and Detached Flights. A principal function of the ATC is to provide flying experience for ATC cadets and for cadets from the Combined Cadet Force (RAF), via the RAF's Air Experience Flights (AEFs) and Volunteer Gliding Schools (VGSs). Twenty-eight such schools make the Air Cadet Gliding Organisation the largest glider training organization in the world.

There are twelve AEFs, parented by the University Air Squadrons and located at RAF St Athan, RAF Boscombe Down, RAF Colerne, Glasgow Airport, RAF Wyton, RAF Benson, RAF Cranwell, RAF Cosford, RAF Church Fenton, RAF Woodvale, RAF Leeming and RAF Leuchars. Their fleet of powered aircraft comprises Grob G115E Tutors. The AEFs' aim is to give each eligible ATC or CCF cadet an annual flight of 20–25 minutes.

The Air Cadet Gliding Organization has a fleet of fifty-three Grob G.109B Vigilant Mk 1s and eighty Grob 103 Viking gliders. The fleet is dispersed at the Air Corps Central Gliding School at RAF Syerston and at the Volunteer

Gliding Schools listed here. Each year, some 1,200 ATC and CCF cadets complete glider training to solo standard, and gain their wings (after their sixteenth birthday) on the Air Cadets Gliding Organisation fleet. Another 1,400 cadets complete an initial gliding course and gain their wings.

ATC Gliding Schools

Number of school	Location
Central Gliding School	Syerston, Nottinghamshire
611 VGS	Stanta Airfield, Norfolk
612 VGS	Abingdon, Oxfordshire
613 VGS	Halton, Buckinghamshire
614 VGS	Halton, Buckinghamshire
615 VGS	Kenley, Surrey
616 VGS	Henlow, Bedfordshire
618 VGS	Odiham, Hampshire
621 VGS	Hullavington, Wiltshire
622 VGS	Upavon, Wiltshire
624 VGS	Chivenor, Devon
625 VGS	Hullavington, Wiltshire
626 VGS	Predannack, Cornwall
631 VGS	Woodvale, Merseyside
632 VGS	Ternhill, Shropshire
633 VGS	Cosford, Shropshire
634 VGS	St Athan, South Glamorgan
635 VGS	Salmesbury, Lancashire
636 VGS	Swansea, West Glamorgan
637 VGS	Little Rissington, Gloucestershire
642 VGS	Linton-on-Ouse, Yorkshire
643 VGS	Syerston, Nottinghamshire
644 VGS	Syerston, Nottinghamshire
645 VGS	Topcliffe, North Yorkshire
661 VGS	Kirknewton, Lothian
663 VGS	Kinloss, Morayshire
664 VGS	Newtownards, Northern Ireland

Besides the AEFs and Volunteer Gliding Schools, the ATC operates several other schemes for getting cadets into the air. An Opportunity Flights Scheme provides many cadets with the opportunity to fly in a variety of RAF aircraft, including fast jets. These usually occur during annual camps, when cadets visit RAF stations. An Overseas Flights Scheme provides an opportunity for cadets to travel on RAF transport flights, usually on routes to Cyprus, Germany and Gibraltar. For some time, there was an arrangement with commercial airlines, allowing cadets to 'sit in' on scheduled services. Unfortunately, the terrorist attacks on New York on 11 September 2001 led to the suspension of these, but it is to be hoped that they will be reinstated at some point in the future.

An important flying scheme offered to air cadets is the Air Cadet Pilot Scheme. Every year, this awards 190 flying courses to successful applicants. The courses themselves comprise 125 Light Aircraft Courses, twenty-five Microlight Courses and forty Air Experience Flying Courses. The Light Aircraft Course provides twelve hours of free flying instruction at Tayside Aviation, Dundee, leading to first solo; the Microlight Course comprises ten hours of flying at RAF Halton, again with the object of attaining first solo. The Air Experience Flying Courses are flown in Grob Tutor aircraft at a number of locations around the country. Another flying opportunity that is open to cadets is the Air Cadet Pilot Navigation Training Course, which provides a two-week course, including ten hours of flying training, on the Tutor with an AEF.

The most valuable flying scheme open to air cadets is the annual Royal Air Forces Association (RAFA) Flying Scholarship. This is open to both male and female air cadets, and offers a course of flying in light aircraft, the primary purpose of which is to encourage participants to go on to obtain an NPPL. The broad requirements are that applicants should have reached the age of seventeen years by the start of their training courses, which are conducted between June and October; should hold GCSE or equivalent passes in English language, mathematics and three other subjects, only one of which may be non-academic; and can take up the offer of training within twelve months. Sixteen finalists undergo pre-assessment screening at the Officer and Aircrew Selection Centre (OASC) at RAF Cranwell, where medical fitness, and personal and pilot aptitudes are examined, although not to the same standard required for entry into the RAF as aircrew. Those who pass the OASC selection procedure enter the Final Selection Competition. The winning cadet is awarded thirty-five hours of free flying instruction in modern light training aircraft, while four runners-up each receive twelve hours of flying training. They may then continue with their training at their own expense to complete the necessary hours for the issue of an NPPL. The training itself is carried out at a number of selected civilian flying schools around the country.

In addition to these courses, which are offered specifically to air cadets, there are a number of bursaries and scholarships offered by the Royal Aero Club, Guild of Air Pilots and Air Navigators, and the Air League for which cadets qualify as young men and women.

THE ROYAL NAVY

Royal Navy admissions for trainee pilots are scarce, and applicants are short-listed to only the very best, even before being seen by the interview board. The rumour that successful applicants are capable of flight with or without an aircraft is officially denied.

However, like commercial pilot vacancies, these gluts and shortages can be cyclical. Do not be deterred from investigating the current situation. Like the RAF, the RN has a two-tier system for recruiting aircrew officers, either by direct application to the Britannia Royal Naval College at Dartmouth in Devon or by university sponsorship. Nationality requirements are the same as those for the RAF detailed previously, but the RN's entry-age limit for trainee pilots is 17–26 years, and candidates must also be at least 151.5cm tall. Initial aptitude testing for would-be navy pilots is again conducted at the OASC at RAF Cranwell, and is followed by a two-day selection session with the Admiralty Interview Board at HMS *Sultan* (a shore base, not a ship) at Gosport in Hampshire. Those candidates recommended for a commission undergo a medical examination before the final selection of short-listed applicants is made.

Those recruits who enter the service via the Britannia Royal Naval College assume the rank of Midshipman. Graduates take the rank of Acting Sub-Lieutenant. Both categories of entrant follow the same initial training pattern, spending two and a half terms at Britannia Naval College, Dartmouth, undergoing practical training at sea, and gaining air experience with the Royal Naval Flying Training Flight on Grob trainers at Plymouth Airport before starting their Elementary Flying Training (EFT) course at the Defence Elementary Flying Training School, RAF Cranwell. The DEFT course lasts for eight months, the first six weeks of which are taken up with

The Royal Navy's Harriers are due to be replaced by the American-designed STOVL F-35 Joint Strike Fighter, built by Lockheed Martin in collaboration with Northrop Grumman and BAE. This aircraft will equip two new, larger aircraft carriers. The F-35 will also replace the RAF's Harrier fleet.
(US Dept of Defense)

The Westland Sea King continues to do sterling service with the Royal Navy. This example is an AEW2, equipped with search radar in a swivelling radome. Sea Kings are also used by the Royal Navy for search and rescue, and as tactical military helicopters for transporting Royal Marine Commandos. (US Dept of Defense)

ground-school studies. The actual flying is conducted at RAF Barkston Heath, where students receive sixty hours (fifteen hours solo) of training on the Slingsby Firefly. The first twenty hours are spent on general handling and are followed by ten hours of navigation instruction. The remainder of the hours are spent on instrument flying and formation flying, after which students take a Final Handling Test. At this point, pilots are streamed for the type of aircraft for which they are best suited: fast jets or helicopters.

Because the number of fixed-wing, carrier-based aircraft in the RN's inventory has been much reduced in recent years, most Fleet Air Arm pilots now fly helicopters, and there are limited opportunities for fixed-wing pilots for the Harrier short take-off/vertical-landing (STOVL) jets that serve aboard the RN's three aircraft carriers, HMS *Illustrious*, *Invincible* and *Ark Royal*. However, plans exist for the construction of two new, larger aircraft carriers, which are likely to be equipped with not only Harriers, but also the STOVL version of the Lockheed Martin F-35 Joint Strike Fighter. Consequently, there may be a greater need for naval fast-jet pilots in future.

Royal Navy pilots streamed for fast-jet flying progress to RAF Linton-on-Ouse, where they complete the same course as their RAF counterparts on the Tucano, before proceeding to RAF Valley for advanced flying instruction and weapons training on BAE Hawks, biased to the operational roles of the Harrier. On completion of the course, students who display the necessary attributes of a Harrier pilot move to RAF Wittering for the final stage of their flying training on the STOVL aircraft.

Would-be helicopter pilots progress to a six-month course at the Defence Helicopter Flying School, RAF Shawbury. This begins with a three-week helicopter ground school. After that, students start flying the Squirrel HT1. Once students have converted successfully to helicopter flying, they continue their training with instruction in instrument flying, navigation, winching, captaincy exercises, and mountain and formation flying. On completion of the course, they are streamed for the specific helicopter for which they are considered suited – Merlin, Lynx or Sea King – and the role that they will play: anti-submarine, search-and-rescue, commando assault or ground attack.

A Flying Badge is awarded to those who successfully complete their initial training phases, usually about ten months after the start of flying training. New pilot entrants can expect to reach operational status with the RN some thirty months after joining the service. Aircrew are not normally permitted to leave the service until at least five years after the award of their Flying Badge.

All aircrew officers join the RN on an Initial Commission, which lasts for twelve years. Promotion within the RN is not tied to any particular stage in pilot training. A Midshipman entrant is promoted to Sub-Lieutenant (Acting or Confirmed status according to whether flying training has been completed or not) after two years' service. He or she should reach the rank of Lieutenant some five years after entry, although this can be reduced if seniority gains have been won during training. Graduates, who assume the rank of Acting Sub-Lieutenant, are confirmed in that rank on completion of operational flying training, unless they have already won promotion to Lieutenant in the meantime. There are opportunities for officers holding an Initial Commission to convert to a Career Commission, which would take them to eighteen years of service, and then to a Full Career Commission with the possibility of continuing to retirement at age fifty-five. Further promotion to Lieutenant-Commander and beyond is competitive, on merit.

THE BRITISH ARMY

Unlike the RN and RAF, the Army employs non-commissioned officer (NCO) aircrew as well as officers, and they make up two thirds of the total pilot complement. They are recruited from all regiments, arms and services of the Army, including the Army Air Corps (AAC). No soldier can enlist directly as aircrew because, before volunteering, they are required to have a proven soldierly track record and to have earned their commanding officer's recommendation. To this end, they must have at least four years' service and have attained a minimum rank of Lance Corporal, with an unequivocal recommendation for promotion to Corporal. They are not required to have any certificated eduation qualifications, but they undergo the same aptitude and medical tests as RAF fast-jet pilots, and identical written and interview acceptance tests as serving Army officers. The last include maths, military knowledge, basic engineering principles, map reading and signals. The selection board is looking for a bright, intelligent soldier, well experienced and versed in Army life and procedures, and with the character and personality to live up to a demanding role. Although officers have previously passed a Regular Commission Board, they, too, go through exactly the same tests as the NCOs.

Having found the right personalities, they are then put through Flying Grading, which is conducted at the School of Army Aviation, Middle Wallop. This entails thirteen hours of fixed-wing flying on the Slingsby Firefly 160, under very experienced instruction to see whether they can learn and retain flying skills and knowledge fast enough to get through the Army Pilot Course. Those NCOs who pass the Pilot Selection Board are loaded on to the Army Pilot Course, but serving officers have yet another hurdle to cross, as they are placed in order of merit for the limited number of vacancies. After that, both officers and NCOs go through the same pilot training.

The selection process is rigorous. Of those who pass through the first filter – their commanding officer's recommendation – some thirty per cent fall by the wayside on aptitude or medical grounds. Of those who start Flying Grading, fewer than fifty per cent are chosen. Even then, some 15–20 per cent are unsuccessful on the Army Pilot Course. Those who pass have most assuredly earned their wings.

NCO pilots come from two main sources, either from within the AAC or on secondment from other regiments or corps within the Army. Both are regarded without let or favour by the selection board. Because they are not involved in the same staff and command structure, NCOs tend to build up more flying hours and pure flying experience than officers.

The AAC soldiers' careers start at the Army Training Regiment, Winchester, where they undergo the fourteen-week Common Military Syllabus Recruits Course. After this, they move to Middle Wallop for a three-week AAC induction course. This is followed by three training modules, covering ground crewman skills (three weeks), signals (four weeks), and aircraft refuelling and hazardous materials training (three weeks). At the end of these courses, the soldiers are sent to the Defence School of Transport at Leconfield, where they learn to maintain and drive the vehicles employed by the AAC. After this, they are classified as AAC Soldiers Class 3 and are ready to be posted to their first regiment.

The AAC accepts both male and female soldiers. Women are expected to perform the same duties as their male counterparts and are treated equally with regard to career development.

There are two means of entry for Army officers: either as Direct Entry (DE) officers or by secondment from another regiment or corps in the Army. Applicants may be male or female. Direct Entry officers begin with a Short Service Commission (SSC), which is for a minimum of six years, although

A British Army Lynx helicopter operating over Bosnia. The Lynx is a multi-role helicopter capable of a variety of battlefield tasks, including fire support using machine guns, troop transport and casualty evacuation. (US Dept of Defense)

this may be extended to a maximum of eight years, depending upon the needs of the Army. SSC officers may apply for an Intermediate Regular Commission (IRC) after serving for two years. This provides an eighteen-year career, which qualifies for a pension. Entrants may be university graduates or accepted direct from school, provided they have the minimum educational qualifications of five GCSE subjects at Grade C or equivalent and two A levels. Maths and English language must be included. Candidates with the minimum educational achievements are seldom considered unless they have other attributes, as competition for Direct Entry is fierce.

The age range for DE commissions is 17½–27 years at entry to RMAS. All DE candidates attend a two-day aircrew aptitude assessment and medical at RAF Cranwell, and a three-week, fourteen-hour Flying Grading Course at the School of Army Aviation (SAAvn) after the RCB. Successful candidates continue to RMAS. Following a year in training at RMAS, DE AAC officers may be required to spend a short time as a subaltern with the Royal Armoured Corps or the Infantry before reporting to the SAAvn for their pilot course.

Candidates who successfully pass the Flying Grading Course are allocated a vacancy on the next available Army Pilot Course, which lasts eighteen months and involves 206 hours of flying. The first phase of training is four weeks of ground school at RAF Cranwell, where students are taught the building blocks of aviation, such as meteorology, principles of flight, aircraft operation and navigation. This is followed by fourteen weeks and forty hours of elementary (fixed-wing) flying on the Firefly 260 at RAF Barkston Heath, to teach airmanship, precision and accuracy, the ability to recover from unusual attitudes, navigation and an introduction to instrument flying.

During this period, pilots make their first solo flight. Next is a week of medical and survival training at RNAS Yeovilton, Lee-on-Solent and Plymouth.

The next phase of the course is Basic Rotary Training, which takes place at the Defence Helicopter Flying School, RAF Shawbury. This begins with three weeks of basic helicopter ground school, covering turbine theory, hydraulics and principles of helicopter flight. The flying training entails thirty-six hours over 8–10 weeks and is conducted on the single-engine Squirrel HT1. Students are taught basic flying techniques, take-offs, landings, circuits, hovering, sloping-ground landings, advanced transitions, quick stops and practice emergencies. Some of their flying will be solo.

Students continue the course at the DHFS with Advanced Rotary Training, which begins with another week of ground school. This is followed by 8–10 weeks of flying training on the Squirrel, being taught such skills as instrument flying, night flying, map reading, low-level navigation and flight in confined areas. At this stage, students will be competent helicopter pilots and ready to move on to Operational Training.

The Operational Training part of the course takes place at Middle Wallop, where the aim is to turn helicopter pilots into Army pilots. It begins with a week of tactics training. Again, instruction is carried out on the Squirrel and involves eighty-eight hours of flying, during which pilots practise night flying wearing night-vision goggles and carry out low-level navigation exercises at tactical heights, including 'nap-of-the-earth' flying. Among other things, they are taught how to direct artillery fire while flying, using live rounds. The aim of this stage of the course is to polish their skills so that they can concentrate on map reading and the tactical situation while flying the aircraft safely. Upon successful completion of the course, pilots are awarded the Army Flying Badge or 'wings'.

After 'wings', pilots will convert on to an operational helicopter type, such as the Gazelle, Lynx or Apache AH1. The Gazelle conversion course takes seven weeks, the Lynx nine weeks and the Apache six months. Following conversion training, newly qualified pilots are posted to AAC regiments for a 2–3-year tour of duty. Each will become the pilot in a crew of two; the other crew member is the Aircraft Commander, who is responsible for 'fighting' the aircraft as well as its safety when flying. After achieving the required experience and having demonstrated the appropriate qualities, pilots will be eligible for appointment as Aircraft Commanders as suitable vacancies occur. Depending on their role and additional duties, officers and NCO pilots with the AAC can expect to log between 600 and 1,000 flying hours during their tour of duty.

IN CIVVY STREET

What are the prospects for military pilots when they leave the services? Overall, they are very good, with demand for former service fliers by airlines and flying training establishments. Foreign governments, particularly those in

The Boeing/Westland AH1 Apache is the latest addition to the Army's helicopter force. This battlefield helicopter is equipped with mast-mounted fire-control radar and a thermal imaging system. It can carry a variety of armaments, including a 30mm cannon, sixteen air-to-ground missiles, four air-to-air missiles and seventy-six rockets.

the Middle East with friendly relations with Britain and British aircraft manufacturers, also place high value on former UK military personnel, and accordingly offer attractive short-term employment packages to those suitably qualified.

All three British armed forces demand minimum commitments of anything from six years upwards, which is entirely reasonable considering the immense cost of training. On leaving the services, resettlement grants are payable, which many ex-military pilots use to gain the civilian flying licences essential to obtain employment in the commercial field, no matter what military qualifications may be held. Professional flying schools run specially developed courses for ex-service aircrew, who are usually permitted to count qualifying flight time logged in the forces toward an exemption from the full CPL course. The CAA will advise on specific requirements necessary in each individual case to gain the civilian licences or ratings. General information is given in the CAA publication *LASORS*.

Bear in mind, however, that as a reason for seeking a service career, the prospect of subsequently getting a civilian flying job is unlikely to endear candidates to selection boards! That said, the Royal Navy does point out in some of its promotional material that its training is of great benefit to ex-naval pilots seeking a commercial flying qualification.

Chapter 6
Contact Names
and Addresses

UK Private Pilot Licence Training Schools and Clubs   Page
    Fixed-wing   106
    Helicopters   129
Professional Pilot Flight Training Schools – UK   137
CAA Approved Overseas Flight Training Schools   138
British Airlines, Scheduled, Charter and Cargo Operators   139
Contact Addresses
    Private, Commercial and Airline Pilots   145
    Military Pilots   146
Pilot Publications and Equipment Retailers   148
Contact Addresses – Aviation Related   150

You are recommended to telephone or check the internet before contacting any of the following organizations. Although all of them have been individually checked at the time of going to press, an organization may have moved or ceased to exist. Writing before checking may result in a long, agonizing wait for a reply that is not going to come. In particular, with an application for employment or sponsorship, checking the address and correct name of an individual who will be dealing with your application is essential. Selection boards have been known to reject applications when it is evident that the candidate has not taken the time and trouble to check that the details are correct. Note that many airlines will only accept employment applications via their web sites.

UK Private Pilot Licence Training Schools and Clubs – Fixed-wing Aircraft

Many of the following organizations also offer training for the National Private Pilot Licence with SSEA rating. Note, however, that due to space considerations, it has not been possible to list establishments that offer training for the NPPL with microlight or SLMG rating. For information on such training, contact either the British Microlight Aircraft Association or British Gliding Association (*see* page 150).

AVON
Bristol and Wessex Aircraft Club, Bristol International Airport, Southside, Lulsgate, Bristol, Somerset BS48 3EP.
Telephone: 01275 474868 E-mail: info@bristolandwessex.co.uk
www.bristolandwessex.co.uk

Bristol Flying Centre, Bristol Airport, Bristol, Somerset BS48 3DT.
Telephone: 01275 474601 E-mail: cfi@b-f-c.co.uk
www.b-f-c.co.uk

BEDFORDSHIRE
Billins Air Services, Building 187, Cranfield Aerodrome, Cranfield, Bedfordshire MK43 0AL.
Telephone: 01234 751400 E-mail: ops@billinsair.freeserve.co.uk
www.billinsair.freeserve.co.uk

Bonus Aviation, Cranfield Aerodrome, Cranfield, Bedfordshire MK43 0JR.
Telephone: 01234 751800 E-mail: info@bonusaviation.co.uk
www.bonusaviation.co.uk

Cabair College of Air Training, Cranfield Aerodrome, Cranfield, Bedfordshire MK43 0JR.
Telephone: 01234 751243 E-mail: cranfield@cabair.com
www.cabairflyingschools.com

Eagle Flight Training, Hangar 129, Prince Way, London Luton Airport, Luton, Bedfordshire LU2 9PD
Telephone: 01582 720007 E-mail: shauneagle@aol.com
www.eagleflight.co.uk

Flyteam Aviation, Building 176, Cranfield Airport, Bedfordshire MK43 0JR.
Telephone: 01234 757728
www.flyteam.com

J S Aviation, Hangar 125, Percival Way, London Luton Airport, Luton, Bedfordshire LU2 9NQ.
Telephone: 01582 726760

Skyline School of Flying, Little Gransden Airfield, Fullers Hill Farm, Gransden, Bedfordshire SG19 3BP.
Telephone: 01767 651950 E-mail: graham@skyline.flyer.co.uk
www.skyline.flyer.co.uk

BERKSHIRE
West London Aero Club, White Waltham Airfield, Maidenhead, Berkshire SL6 3NJ.
Telephone: 01628 823272 E-mail: ops@wlac.co.uk
www.wlac.co.uk

BUCKINGHAMSHIRE
British Airways Flying Club, Wycombe Air Park, Booker, Marlow, Buckinghamshire SL7 3DP.
Telephone: 01494 529262 E-mail: info@bafc.co.uk
www.bafc.co.uk

The Pilot Centre, Denham Aerodrome, Uxbridge, Middlesex UB9 5DF.
Telephone: 01895 833838 E-mail: pilot.centre@lineone.net

Wycombe Air Centre, Wycombe Air Park, Booker, Marlow, Buckinghamshire SL7 3DR.
Telephone: 01494 443737 E-mail: info@wycombeaircentre.co.uk
www.wycombeaircentre.co.uk

CAMBRIDGESHIRE
Cambridge Aero Club, The Airport, Newmarket Road, Cambridge CB5 8RX.
Telephone: 01223 373214 E-mail: pilots@marshallaerospace.com
www.cambridgeaeroclub.co.uk

Cambridge Flying Group, The Airport, Newmarket Road, Cambridge CB5 8RX.
Telephone: 01223 293343 E-mail: info@cambridgeflyinggroup.co.uk
www.cambridgeflyinggroup.co.uk

Flying Club Conington, Erwin House, Peterborough Business Airfield, Holme, Peterborough, Cambridgeshire PE7 3PX.
Telephone: 01487 834161 E-mail: info@flying-club-conington.co.uk
www.flying-club-conington.co.uk

Mid-Anglia School of Flying, The Airport, Newmarket Road, Cambridge CB5 8RX.
Telephone: 01223 294466 E-mail: masfcambridge@aol.com
www.masfcambridge.com

NSF Sibson, Sibson Aerodrome, Wansford, Peterborough, Cambridgeshire PE8 6NE.
Telephone: 01832 280289 E-mail: info@nsof.co.uk
www.nsof.co.uk

Rural Flying Corps, Bourn Aerodrome, Cambridge, Cambridgeshire CB3 7TQ.
Telephone: 01954 719602 E-mail: info@rfcbourn.flyer.co.uk
www.rfcbourn.flyer.co.uk

CHANNEL ISLANDS
Alderney Flying Training, States Airport Alderney GY9 3AJ.
Telephone: 01481 823053 E-mail: contact@flyalderney.com
www.flyalderney.com

Guernsey Aero Club, States Airport, Guernsey, Channel Islands GY8 0DS.
Telephone: 01481 265254 E-mail: manager@guernseyaeroclub.com
www.guernseyaeroclub.com

Jersey Aero Club, States Airport, St Peter, Jersey, Channel Islands JE3 7BP.
Telephone: 01534 743990 E-mail: info@jerseyaeroclub.com
www.jerseyaeroclub.com

CORNWALL
Cornwall Flying Club, Bodmin Airfield, Cardinham, Bodmin, Cornwall PL30 4BU
Telephone: 01208 821419 E-mail: fly@cornwallflyingclub.com
www.cornwallflyingclub.com

Land's End Flying School, Land's End Aerodrome, St Just, Penzance TR19 7RL.
Telephone: 01736 788771 E-mail: flyingschool@islesofscilly-travel.co.uk

Perranporth Flying School, Perranporth Airfield, Higher Trevellas, St Agnes, Cornwall TR5 0XS.
Telephone: 01872 552266
www.perranporthairfield.com

COUNTY DURHAM
Cleveland Flying School, Durham Tees Valley Airport, Darlington, County Durham DL2 1NW.
Telephone: 01325 332855 E-mail: craig.mcleod@northern-aviation.com
www.clevelandflying.co.uk

St George Flight Training, Durham Tees Valley Airport, Darlington, County Durham DL2 1NL.
Telephone: 01325 333431 E-mail: info@stgeorgeflighttraining.co.uk
www.stgeorgeflighttraining.co.uk

CUMBRIA

Border Air Training, Hangar 30, Carlisle Airport, Crosby in Eden, Carlisle CA6 4NW.
Telephone: 01228 573490 E-mail: info@borderairtraining.com
www.borderairtraining.com

Carlisle Flight Training, Hangar 30, Carlisle Airport, Crosby-on-Eden, Cumbria CA6 4NW.
Telephone: 01228 573344 E-mail: info@carlisle-flight-training.com
www.carlisle-flight-training.com

DERBYSHIRE

Derby Aero Club & Flying School, Derby Airfield, Hilton Road, Egginton, Derbyshire DE65 6GU.
Telephone: 01283 733803 E-mail: derbyaeroclub@btinternet.com

Donair Flying Club, Building 33, Dakota Road, East Midlands Airport, Castle Donington, Derbyshire DE74 2SA.
Telephone: 01332 810444 E-mail: info@donaireastmidlands.co.uk
www.donair.co.uk

East Midlands Flying School, Building 120, East Midlands Airport, Castle Donington, Derby DE74 2SA.
Telephone: 01332 850383
E-mail: info@donaireastmidlands.co.uk

DEVON

Ace Flight Training, 24 Walcott Way,
Dunkeswell, Honiton, Devon EX14 4XP.
Telephone: 01404 891811 E-mail: info@aceflight.co.uk
www.aceflight.co.uk

Advanced Flight, Flymore, Hangar 3, Dunkeswell Aerodrome, Honiton, Devon EX14 4LT.
Telephone: 01404 891504

Aviation South West, Building 26, Exeter Airport, Clyst Honiton, Exeter, Devon EX5 2BD.
Telephone: 01392 447887 E-mail: info@egte.com
www.egte.com

Devon & Somerset Flight Training, Dunkeswell Aerodrome, Dunkeswell, Honiton, Devon EX14 4LG.
Telephone: 01404 891643 E-mail: info@dsft.co.uk
home.btconnect.com/dsft/

Eaglescott School of Flying, Eaglescott Airfield, Burrington, North Devon EX37 9LH.
Telephone: 01769 520404
www.eaglescott-airfield.com

Exeter Flying Club, Exeter Airport, Clyst Honiton, Exeter, Devon EX5 2BA.
Telephone: 01392 367653 E-mail: info@flying-club.com
www.flying-club.com

Plymouth Flying School, Plymouth City Airport, Crown Hill, Plymouth, Devon PL6 8BW.
Telephone: 01752 773335 E-mail: fly@plymouthflyingschool.co.uk
www.plymouthflyingschool.co.uk

DORSET
Airbourne Aviation, Popham Airfield, Micheldever, Hampshire SO43 3HB.
Telephone: 01256 398254 (office)/01202 822486 (airfield)

Bournemouth Flying Club, Aviation Park East, Bournemouth International Airport, Christchurch, Dorset BH23 6NE.
Telephone: 01202 578558
E-mail: ian.huntley@bournemouthflyingclub.co.uk
www.bournemouthflyingclub.co.uk

Cabair College of Air Training, Bournemouth International Airport, Christchurch, Dorset BH23 6NW.
Telephone: 01202 581122 E-mail: Bournemouth@cabair.com
www.cabairflyingschools.com

FR Aviation Flying Club, Bournemouth International Airport, Christchurch, Dorset BH23 6NE.
Telephone: 01202 409000

Professional Air Training, Oakland House, Building 420, Aviation Park West, Bournemouth International Airport, Christchurch, Dorset BH23 6NW.
Telephone: 01202 593366 E-mail: info@pat.uk.com
www.pat.uk.com

Solent School of Flying, Building 6000, Bournemouth International Airport, Christchurch, Dorset BH23 6SE.
Telephone: 01202 582181 E-mail: info@bourne2fly.co.uk
www.solentsf.co.uk

ESSEX

Anglian Flight Centres, Earls Colne Airfield, Earls Colne, Colchester, Essex CO6 2NS.
Telephone: 01787 223676 E-mail: enquiries@flyafc.co.uk
www.anglianflightcentres.co.uk

Andrewsfield Aviation, Saling Airfield, Great Dunmow, Essex CM6 3TH.
Telephone: 01371 856744 E-mail: info@andrewsfield.com
www.andrewsfield.com

Clacton Aero Club, Clacton Airfield, West Road, Clacton-on-sea, Essex CO15 1AG.
Telephone: 01255 424671 E-mail: info@clactonaeroclub.co.uk
www.clactonaeroclub.co.uk

Colchester Flying Club, Nonsuch House, 1 East Street, Wivenhoe, Essex CO7 9BW.
Telephone: 01206 823879

Seawing Flying Club, Eastern Perimeter Road, Southend Airport, Southend-on-Sea, Essex SS2 6YF.
Telephone: 01702 545420 E-mail: seawingfc@aol.com
www.seawingfc.co.uk

Southend Flying Club, Southend Airport, Cargo Entrance, South Road, Southend-on-Sea, Essex SS2 6YF.
Telephone: 01702 545198 E-mail: youfly@southendflying club.co.uk
www.southendflyingclub.co.uk

Stapleford Flight Centre, Stapleford Aerodrome, Romford, Essex RM4 1SJ.
Telephone: 01708 688380 E-mail: postmaster@flysfc.com
www.flysfc.com

Willowair Flying Club, Eastern Perimeter Road, London Southend Airport, Southend-on-Sea, Essex SS2 6YF.
Telephone: 01702 531555 E-mail: sales@willowair.co.uk
www.willoair.co.uk

GLOUCESTERSHIRE

Aero GB, Hanger SE 7, Gloucestershire Airport, Cheltenham, Gloucestershire GL51 6SP.
Telephone: 07718 585645 E-mail: robinsmall@aerogb.com
www.aerogb.com

Aeros Flying Club, Building SE 4, Gloucestershire Airport, Cheltenham, Gloucestershire GL51 6SP.
Telephone: 01452 857419 E-mail: aerosfc@aol.com
www.aeros.co.uk

BCT Aviation, D Site, Kemble Flight Centre, Kemble Airfield, Kemble, Gloucestershire GL7 6BA.
Telephone: 01285 771015 E-mail: ops@bctaviation.com

Cotswold Aero Club, Gloucestershire Airport, Cheltenham, Gloucestershire GL51 6SF.
Telephone: 01452 713924 E-mail: phil@cotswoldaeroclub.com
www.cotswoldaeroclub.com

The Flying Club, The Old Fire Station, Kemble Aerodrome, Kemble, Gloucestershire GL7 6BA.
Telephone: 01285 771025 E-mail: bookings@theflyingclubkemble.com
www.theflyingclubkemble.com

Gloucestershire & Cheltenham School of Flying, Building SE 4, Gloucestershire Airport, Cheltenham, Gloucestershire GL51 6SP.
Telephone: 01452 857153

Skysport UK (Andrewsfield), Three Ways Cottage, Ampney Crucis, Gloucestershire GL7 5RZ.
Telephone: 01285 851311 E-mail: rogerhayes@dial.pipex.com
Dspace.dial.pipex.com/skysport/

Skytime Flight Training, Firfax Building, Meteor Business Park, Cheltenham Road East, Gloucestershire Airport, Cheltenham, Gloucestershire GL2 9QL.
Telephone: 01452 857420 E-mail: info@skytime.co.uk
www.skytime.co.uk

Staverton Flying School, Gloucestershire Airport, Cheltenham, Gloucestershire GL51 6ST.
Telephone: 01452 712388 E-mail: info@stavertonflyingschool.co.uk
www.stavertonflyingschool.co.uk

GREATER MANCHESTER
Flight Academy, Block A, Barton Airfield, Liverpool Road, Eccles, Manchester M30 7SA.
Telephone: 0161 788 8489 E-mail: info@flightacademy.co.uk
www.flightsandlessons.com

JD Aviation, Business Aviation Centre, Hangar 7, Manchester Airport West, Manchester M90 5NE.
Telephone: 0161 436 0125 E-mail: fly@jd-aviation.co.uk
www.jd-aviation.co.uk

MSF Aviation, Airside, Aviation Viewing Park, Manchester Airport, Manchester M90 1QX.
Telephone: 0161 436 2222 E-mail: ops@msfaviation.com
www.msfaviation.com

HAMPSHIRE
Carill Aviation, HMS *Daedalus*, Broomway, Lee-on-Solent, Hampshire PO13 9YA.
Telephone: 02392 553310 E-mail: enquiries@carillaviation.co.uk
www.carillaviation.co.uk

Solent Flight, Lower Upham Airfield, Winchester Road, Bishops Waltham, Hampshire SO32 1BZ.
Telephone: 01489 861333 E-mail: mail@solentflight.com
www.solentflight.com

Spitfire Flying Club, Popham Airfield, Micheldever, Winchester, Hampshire SO21 3BD.
Telephone: 01253 397733 E-mail: pophamairfield@aol.com
www.popham-airfield.com

Western Air (Thruxton), Thruxton Airfield, Andover, Hampshire SP11 8PW.
Telephone: 01264 773900 E-mail: westernair@thruxtonairport.com
www.westernairthruxton.co.uk

HEREFORDSHIRE
Herefordshire Aero Club, Shobdon Airfield, Nr Leominster, Herefordshire HR6 9NR.
Telephone: 01568 708369 E-mail: hac@aeroclub.co.uk
www.aeroclub.co.uk

HERTFORDSHIRE
Chiltern Aviation, Elstree Aerodrome, Hertfordshire WD6 3AR.
Telephone: 0468 207207

East Herts Flying School, Panshanger Aerodrome, Cole Green, Hertfordshire SG14 2NH
Telephone: 01707 391791 E-mail: info@northlondonflyingschool.com
www.northlondonflyingschool.com

Firecrest Aviation, Elstree Aerodrome, Borehamwood, Hertfordshire WD6 3AW.
Telephone: 020 8207 6201 E-mail: enquiries@firecrestaviation.co.uk
www.firecrestaviation.co.uk

Flyteam Aviation, Control Tower Building, Elstree Aerodrome, Borehamwood, Hertfordshire WD6 3AW.
Telephone: 020 8381 8899 E-mail: enquiries@flyteam.com
www.flyteam.com

London School of Flying (Cabair), Elstree Aerodrome, Borehamwood, Hertfordshire WD6 3AW.
Telephone: 020 8953 4343 E-mail: lsf@cabair.com
www.cabairflyingschools.com

MAK Aviation, Elstree Aerodrome, Borehamwood, Hertfordshire WD6 3AW.
Telephone: 020 8363 8290

Modern Air, Fowlmere Aerodrome, Royston, Hertfordshire SG8 7SJ.
Telephone: 01763 208281 E-mail: dg@modair.co.uk
home.btconnect.com/modair/

HUMBERSIDE – *see also* entries under **YORKSHIRE**
Triple 'A' Flying, The Flight House, Kirmington Vale, Barnetby, South Humberside DN38 6AF.
Telephone: 01652 680564 E-mail: info@tripleaflying.co.uk
www.tripleaflying.co.uk

ISLE OF MAN
Ashley Gardner School of Flying, Hangar 2, Ronaldsway Airport, Ballasalla, Isle of Man IM9 4EW.
Telephone: 01624 823454

Manx Flyers Aero Club, The 27 Clubhouse, Derbyhaven, Castletown, Isle of Man IM9 1TU.
Telephone: 01624 825999 E-mail: manxflyers@manx.net
www.manxflyersaeroclub.com

ISLE OF WIGHT
Bembridge Flight Training School, Isle of Wight Airport, Scotchells Brook Lane, Sandown, Isle of Wight PO36 0JP.
Telephone: 01983 408374 E-mail: bobbler@btinternet.com
www.isleofwightflyingclub.co.uk

Specialist Flying School, Isle of Wight Airport, Embassy Way, Sandown, Isle of Wight PO36 0JP.
Telephone: 01983 402402 E-mail: info@flyingschool.com
www.flyingschool.com

KENT
Airborne Adventures, Headcorn Aerodrome, Headcorn, Kent TN27 9HX.
Telephone: 01622 892002 E-mail: enquiries@airborneadventures.co.uk
www.airborneadventures.co.uk

Alouette Flying Club, Building C700 East Camp, Biggin Hill Airport, Biggin Hill, Kent TN16 3BN
Telephone: 01959 573243
www.alouette.org.uk

Aviation Tutors, Headcorn Aerodrome, Headcorn, Kent TN27 9HX.
Telephone: 01622 891539

Biggin Hill School of Flying (Cabair), Building 165, Biggin Hill Airport, Biggin Hill, Kent TN16 3BN.
Telephone: 01959 573583 E-mail: bigginhill@cabair.com
www.cabairflyingschools.com

Classair, Building C701, Biggin Hill Aerodrome, Biggin Hill, Kent TN16 3BN.
Telephone: 01959 540495 E-mail: iris@classair.co.uk
www.classair.co.uk

Cross Air Aviation, Headcorn Aerodrome, Headcorn, Kent TN27 9HX.
Telephone: 01622 891539

EFG Flying School, Building 164, Biggin Hill Aerodrome, Biggin Hill, Kent TN16 3BN.
Telephone: 01959 540054 E-mail: operations@efgflyer.co.uk
www.flyefg.co.uk

Island Aviation, Eastchurch Airfield, Parsonage Farm, Church Road, Eastchurch, Isle of Sheppey, Kent ME12 4DQ.
Telephone: 01795 881183

Lydd Aero Club, Lydd Airport, Lydd, Romney Marsh, Kent TN29 9QL.
Telephone: 01797 320734 E-mail: lyddaero@btconnect.com
www.lyddaero.co.uk

Medway Flight Training, Farthing Corner Airfield, Stoneacre Farm, Mattshill Road, Hartlip, Nr Sittingbourne, Kent ME9 7XD.
Telephone: 01634 389757 E-mail: mft@avnet.co.uk
www.avnet.co.uk/mft

Millen Aviation Services, Rochester Airport, Maidstone Road, Chatham, Kent ME5 9SD.
Telephone: 01634 200787 E-mail: info@millencorporation.com
www.millencorporation.com

Plane Crazy, Headcorn Aerodrome, Headcorn, Kent TN27 9HX.
Telephone: 01580 895147 E-mail: info@strictlyflying.com

Rochester School of Flying (Cabair), Rochester Airport, Maidstone Road, Chatham, Kent ME5 9SD.
Telephone: 01634 861713 E-mail: rochester@cabair.com
www.cabairflyingschools.com

Surrey & Kent Flying Club, Building 447, Biggin Hill Aerodrome, Biggin Hill, Kent TN16 3BN
Telephone: 01959 540579 E-mail: info@sandk.flyer.co.uk
www.sandk.flyer.co.uk

TG Aviation, Manston Airport, Ramsgate, Kent CT12 5BP.
Telephone: 01843 823656 E-mail: info@tgaviation.com
www.tgaviation.com

Tropair Air Services, Hangar 528, Biggin Hill Airport, Biggin Hill, Kent TN16 3BN.
Telephone: 01959 576767 E-mail: paul@tropair.com
www.tropair.com

Weald Air Services, Headcorn Aerodrome, Headcorn, Kent TN27 9HX.
Telephone: 01622 891539 E-mail: weald.aviatorsclub@freeserve.co.uk

W E Aviation, Rochester Airport South, Maidstone Road, Chatham, Kent ME5 9SD.
Telephone: 01634 861464

LANCASHIRE
ANT Flying Club, Blackpool Airport, Squires Gate Lane, Blackpool FY4 2QS.
Telephone: 01253 345396 E-mail: info@airnav.co.uk
www.airnav.co.uk

Blackpool & Fylde Aero Club, Blackpool Airport, Blackpool FY4 2QS
Telephone: 01253 341871 E-mail: brian@flying60.freeserve.co.uk

Cheshire Air Training School, General Aviation Area, Viscount Drive,
Liverpool Airport, Liverpool L24 5GA
Telephone: 0870 922 0847 E-mail: info@cheshair.co.uk
www.cheshair.co.uk

Flight Academy Blackpool, Blackpool Airport, Blackpool FY4 2QY.
Telephone: 01253 349072 E-mail: crgsvll@aol.com

LAC Flying School, Barton Aerodrome, Liverpool Road, Eccles, Lancashire
M30 7SA.
Telephone: 0161 787 7326 E-mail: 238stu@gmail.com
www.lacflyingschool.co.uk

Liverpool Flying School, Hangar 4, Liverpool Airport North, L24 8QQ
Telephone: 0151 427 7449 E-mail: email@liverpoolflyingschool.com
www.lfs.co.uk

Pool Aviation Flying School, Blackpool Airport, Blackpool FY4 2QY.
Telephone: 01253 407070

Ravenair, Business Aviation Centre, South Terminal, Liverpool Airport,
Liverpool L24 5GA
Telephone: 0151 486 6161 E-mail: ops@ravenair.co.uk
www.ravenair.co.uk

Silverstar Aviation, Hangar 8, Blackpool Airport, Blackpool FY4 2QY.
Telephone: 01253 341010 E-mail: carolinesilverstar@9mail.com

Westair Flying School, Blackpool Airport, Blackpool FY4 2QX.
Telephone: 01253 404925 E-mail: school@westair.uk.com
www.westair.uk.com

LEICESTERSHIRE
Leicestershire Aero Club, Leicester Airport, Leicester LE2 2FG.
Telephone: 0116 259 2360 E-mail: info@leicestershireaeroclub.co.uk
www.leicestershireaeroclub.co.uk

LINCOLNSHIRE
Fenland Flying School, Fenland Airfield, Holbeach St Johns, Spalding,
Lincolnshire PE12 8RQ.
Telephone: 01406 540461 E-mail: info@fenland-flying-school.co.uk
www.fenland-flying-school.co.uk

Fly365, The Control Tower, Wickenby Airfield, Langworth, Lincolnshire LN3 5AX.
Telephone: 01673 885111 E-mail: info@fly365.co.uk
www.fly365.co.uk

Humber Flying Club, 26 Franklin Way, Humberside International Airport, Kirmington, Lincolnshire DN39 6YH.
Telephone: 01652 680746 E-mail: enquiries@humberflyingclub.co.uk
www.humberflyingclub.co.uk

Humberside Flight Training, Plot 25, School Way, Humberside International Airport, Kirmington, Lincolnshire DN39 6YH.
Telephone: 01652 688056 E-mail: fly@humbersideflighttraining.co.uk
www.humbersideflighttraining.co.uk

Lincoln Aero Club, Sturgate Airport, Upton, Gainsborough, Lincolnshire DN21 5PA.
Telephone: 01427 838305 E-mail: lincegcs@aol.com
www.lincolnaeroclub.co.uk

Frank Morgan School of Flying, 13A Hall Way, Humberside International Airport, Kirmington, Lincolnshire DN39 6YH.
Telephone: 01652 688859 E-mail: info@flyatfranks.co.uk
www.flyatfranks.co.uk

Solo Flight, Humberside International Airport, Kirmington, Lincolnshire DN39 6YH.
Telephone: 01652 688833

Wickenby Aviation, Hangar 1, Wickenby Airfield, Langworth, Lincolnshire CN3 5AX.
Telephone: 01673 885345

MIDDLESEX
Denham School of Flying (Cabair), Denham Aerodrome, Uxbridge, Middlesex UB9 5DE.
Telephone: 01895 833327 E-mail: denham@cabair.com
www.cabairflyingschools.com

Lapwing Flying Group, Denham Aerodrome North Side, Uxbridge, Middlesex UB9 5DE.
Telephone: 01895 833880

The Pilot Centre, Denham Aerodrome, Uxbridge, Middlesex UB9 5DF.
Telephone: 01895 833838 E-mail: pilot.centre@lineone.net

NORFOLK

Anglia Flight, Hangar 10, Norwich Airport, Norwich NR6 6EG
Telephone: 01603 412888 E-mail: dale@anglia-flight.co.uk
www.anglia-flight.co.uk

Anglian Air Centre, Hangar 12, Gambling Close, Norwich Airport,
Norwich, Norfolk NR6 6EG.
Telephone: 01603 410866 E-mail: info@anglianaircentre.co.uk
www.anglianaircentre.co.uk

Norwich School of Flying, Liberator Road, Norwich Airport, Norwich
NR6 6EU.
Telephone: 01603 403107 E-mail: brian@nsf.flyer.co.uk
www.nsf.flyer.co.uk

Old Buckenham Aero Club, Old Buckenham Airfield, Abbey Road, Old
Buckenham, Norfolk NK17 1PU.
Telephone: 01953 860806 E-mail: flying@oldbuckaeroclub.com
www.oldbuckaeroclub.com

Premier Flight Training, Gambling Close, Norwich Airport, Norwich NR6
6EG.
Telephone: 01603 414641 E-mail: flying@premierflighttraining.co.uk
www.premierflighttraining.co.uk

Wingtask 1995, Seething Aerodrome, Brooke, Norwich, Norfolk
NR15 1EL.
Telephone: 01508 550453
www.seething-airfield.com

NORTHAMPTONSHIRE

2 Excel Aviation, The Tiger House, Sywell Aerodrome, Northampton,
Northamptonshire NN6 0BN.
Telephone: 01604 671309 E-mail: info@2excelaviation.com
www.2excelaviation.com

Brooklands Flying Club, Shackleton Hangar, Sywell Aerodrome,
Northampton, Northamptonshire NN6 0BN.
Telephone: 01604 496600 E-mail: info@sywellaerodrome.co.uk
www.sywellaerodrome.co.uk/brooklands

Turweston Flying School, Turweston Aerodrome, Brackley,
Northamptonshire NN13 5YD.
Telephone: 01280 701167 E-mail: info@turwestonflyingschool.co.uk
www.turwestonflyingschool.co.uk

NORTHERN IRELAND
Belfast Flying Club, Belfast International Airport, Crumlin, Belfast,
Northern Ireland BT29 4AB
Telephone: 028 9445 2153
www.belfast-flying-club.com

Eglinton Flying Club, 17A Airfield Road, Eglinton, Londonderry,
Northern Ireland BT47 3PZ.
Telephone: 02871 810962 E-mail: info@eglintonflyingclub.com
www.eglintonflyingclub.com

Enniskillen Flying School, Enniskillen (St Angelo) Airport, Trory,
Enniskillen, County Fermanagh, Northern Ireland BT94 2FP.
Telephone: 02866 322077

Ulster Flying Club, Newtownards Airport, PortaferryRoad, County Down,
Northern Ireland BT23 8SG.
Telephone: 02891 813327
www.ulsterflyingclub.com

NOTTINGHAMSHIRE
ALH Skytrain, Retford Gamston Airfield, Nottinghamshire DN22 0QL.
Telephone: 01777 838222 E-mail: tony@skytrain.f9.co.uk

Phoenix Flying School, Netherthorpe Airfield, Thorpe Salvin, Nr Worksop,
Nottinghamshire S80 3JQ.
Telephone: 01909 481802 E-main: phoenix-flying@lineone.net
www.phoenix-flying.co.uk

Sheffield Aero Club, Netherthorpe Airfield, Thorpe Salvin, Nr Worksop,
Nottinghamshire S80 3JQ.
Telephone: 01909 475233 E-mail: info@sheffieldaeroclub.net
www.sheffieldaeroclub.net

Sheffield City Flying School, Sheffield City Airport, Sheffield S9 1XZ.
Telephone: 0114 2923401
www.sheffieldcityflyingschool.net

The Sherwood Flying Club, Nottingham Airport, Tollerton,
Nottinghamshire NG12 4GA.
Telephone: 0115 981 1402

Truman Aviation, Nottingham Airport, Tollerton,
Nottinghamshire NG12 4GA.
Telephone: 0115 981 5050 E-mail: info@trumanaviation.demon.co.uk

OXFORDSHIRE

Air Training Services, Enstone Airfield, Church Enstone, Oxfordshire OX7 4NP.
Telephone: 07961 451565
www.airtrainingservices.com

Enstone Flying Club, Enstone Airfield, Church Enstone, Oxfordshire OX7 4NP.
Telephone: 01608 678204 E-mail: info@enstone-flyingclub.co.uk
www.enstone-flyingclub.co.uk

Oxford Aviation Training, Oxford Airport, Kidlington, Oxford OX5 1QX.
Telephone: 01865 841234 E-mail: oatsmktg@oxfordaviation.net
www.oxfordaviation.net

Pilot Flight Training, 219 Banbury Road, Kidlington, Oxfordshire OX5 1AL.
Telephone: 01865 370814 E-mail: info@pilotflighttraining.com
www.pilotflighttraining.com

SCOTLAND

Cumbernauld Flying School, Cumbernauld Airport, Duncan McIntosh Road, Cumbernauld, Glasgow, Lanarkshire G68 0HH.
Telephone: 01236 452525 E-mail: info@cumbernauldflyingschool.co.uk
www.cumbernauldflyingschool.co.uk

Edinburgh Flying Club, Business Aviation Centre, Edinburgh EH12 9DN.
Telephone: 0131 339 4990 E-mail: info@edinburghflyingclub.co.uk
www.edinburghflyingclub.co.uk

Far North Flight Training, Wick Airport, Caithness, Highland KW1 4QP.
Telephone: 01955 602201

Glasgow Flying Club, Walkinshaw Road, Renfrew, Renfrewshire PA4 9LP.
Telephone: 0141 889 4565 E-mail: info@glasgowflyingclub.com
www.glasgowflyingclub.com

Highland Flying School, North Apron, Inverness Airport, Inverness IN1 7JB.
Telephone: 01667 462226
E-mail: information@highlandflyingschool.co.uk
www.highlandflyingschool.co.uk

Kintyre Aviation, Kildallok, Campbeltown, Argyll PA28 6RE.
Telephone: 01586 553192 E-mail: marycturner@btinternet.com

Leading Edge Flight Training, Cumbernauld Airport, Duncan McIntosh
Road, Cumbernauld, Glasgow, Lanarkshire G68 0HH.
Telephone: 01389 804804
www.fly-le.co.uk

Leading Edge Flight Training, Perth Airport, Perthshire PH2 6PL.
Telephone: 01236 727727
www.fly-le.co.uk

Prestwick Flight Centre, Hangar 22A, Prestwick Airport KA9 2PQ.
Telephone: 01292 476523 E-mail: info@prestwickflightcentre.com
www.prestwickflightcentre.com

Tayside Aviation, Dundee Airport, Riverside Drive, Dundee DD2 1UH
Telephone: 01382 644577 E-mail: enquiries@tayesideaviation.co.uk
www.taysideaviation.co.uk

Tayside Aviation, Fife (Glenrothes) Airport, Goatmilk, Glenrothes, Fife
KY6 2SL.
Telephone: 01592 753792 E-mail: enquiries@taysideaviation.co.uk
www.taysideaviation.co.uk

SHROPSHIRE
Shropshire Aero Club, Sleap Aerodrome, Shropshire SY4 3HE.
Telephone: 01939 232 882 E-mail: info@shropshireaeroclub.com
www.shropshireaeroclub.co.uk

STAFFORDSHIRE
Tatenhill Aviation, Tatenhill Airfield, Newborough Road, Needwood,
Burton-on-Trent, Staffordshire DE13 9PD.
Telephone: 01283 575283 E-mail: mail@tatenhill.com
www.tatenhill.com

SUFFOLK
Crowfield Flying Club, Crowfield Airfield, Coddenham Green, Ipswich,
Suffolk IP6 9UN.
Telephone: 01449 711017

Horizon Flying Club, Monewden Airfield, Monewden, Woodbridge,
Suffolk IP13 7DF.
Telephone: 01473 737677 E-mail: enquiries@horizonflying.com
www.horizonflying.com

Rainair (Beccles), Beccles Airfield, Beccles, Suffolk NR34 7TE
Telephone: 0467 827172 E-mail: info@rainair.co.uk
www.rainair.co.uk

SURREY
Blackbushe Aviation, Blackbushe Airport, Nr Camberley, Surrey
GU17 9LB.
Telephone: 01252 877727 E-mail: info@blackbusheaviation.com
www.blackbusheaviation.co.uk

Blackbushe School of Flying (Cabair), Terminal Building, Blackbushe
Airport, Nr Camberley, Surrey GU17 9LQ.
Telephone: 01252 870999 E-mail: blackbushe@cabair.com
www.cabairflyingschools.com

Cloudbase Aviation Services, Redhill Aerodrome, Crabhill Lane, South
Nutfield, Redhill, Surrey RH1 5JY.
Telephone: 01737 822423 E-mail: cloudbase@mistral.co.uk
www.theflyingschool.co.uk

Cubair Flight Training, Hangar 8, Redhill Aerodrome, Kingsmill Lane,
Redhill, Surrey RH1 5JY.
Telephone: 01737 822124 E-mail: ops@cubair.co.uk
www.cubair.demon.co.uk

Harvard Aviation, Redhill Aerodrome, Terminal Building, Redhill, Surrey
RH1 5YP.
Telephone: 01737 823001 E-mail: info@harvardaviation.com
www.harvardaviation.com

Redhill Aviation, South Block, Redhill Aerodrome, Kingsmill Lane, Surrey
RH1 5JY.
Telephone: 01737 822959 E-mail: islamredhill@aol.com
www.redhillaviation.co.uk

SUSSEX
Flying Time, Wingfield House, Shoreham Airport, Shoreham-by-Sea, West
Sussex BN43 5FF.
Telephone: 01273 455177 E-mail: admin@flyingtime.co.uk
www.flyingtime.co.uk

Goodwood Flying School, Goodwood Airfield, Goodwood, Chichester,
West Sussex P018 0PH.
Telephone: 01243 755066 E-mail: fsd@goodwood.co.uk
www.goodwood.co.uk

Mithril Flying Club, The Old Control Tower, Goodwood Motor Circuit, Chichester, West Sussex PO18 0PH.
Telephone: 01243 528815

The Real Flying Company, 3 Cecil Pashley Way, Shoreham Airport, Shoreham-by-Sea, West Sussex, BN43 5FF.
Telephone: 01273 440288 E-mail: ops@realflyingcompany.com
www.realflyingcompany.com

Sky Leisure Aviation, First Floor, Terminal Building, Shoreham Airport, Shoreham-by-Sea, West Sussex BN43 5FF.
Telephone: 01273 464422 Email: operations@skyleisureaviation.co.uk
www.skyleisureaviation.co.uk

Southern Flying Centre, Main Terminal Building, Shoreham Airport, Shoreham-by-Sea, West Sussex BN43 5FF.
Telephone: 01273 461661 E-mail: ops@southernflyingcentre.co.uk
www.southernflyingcentre.co.uk

Sussex Flying Club, First Floor, Main Terminal Building, Shoreham Airport, Shoreham-by-Sea, West Sussex, BN43 5FF.
Telephone: 01243 440852 E-mail: ops@sfc.ac
www.sfc.ac

TYNE & WEAR
Northumbria Flying School, Newcastle International Airport, Woolsington, Newcastle upon Tyne, Northumberland NE13 8BT.
Telephone: 0191 286 1321
E-mail: admin@northumbria-flying-school.co.uk
www.northumbria-flying-school.co.uk

WALES
Cambrian Flying Club, Medway Building, Haverfordwest SA16 0HZ.
Telephone: 07976 961583 E-mail: info@cambrianflyingclub.co.uk
www.cambrianflyingschool.co.uk

Cardiff Academy of Aviation, The White Building, Cardiff International Airport, Rhoose, South Glamorgan CF62 3BD.
Telephone: 01446 710000
www.cardiffacademyofaviation.co.uk

Haverfordwest School of Flying, Withybush Aerodrome, Fishguard Road, Haverfordwest, Pembrokeshire SA62 4BM.
Telephone: 01437 760822 E-mail: training@flywales.co.uk
www.flywales.co.uk

Horizon Aviation, Swansea Airport, Fairwood Common SA2 7JV.
Telephone: 01792 204063
www.swanseaflyingschool.co.uk

Impulse Aviation, Mid-Wales Airport, Welshpool, Powys SY21 8SG.
Telephone: 01938 554419 E-mail: skilltrain.consulting@virgin.net

Mona Flying Club, RAF Mona, Gwalchmai, Ynys Mon, Anglesey
LL54 5TD.
Telephone: 01407 720581
www.flymona.com

QDM Aviation, Caernarfon Airport, Dis Dinile, Caernarfon LL54 5TP.
Telephone: 01286 830800 E-mail: info@qdm-aviation.co.uk
www.air-world.co.uk

Welshpool Flying School, Mid-Wales Airport, Welshpool SY21 8SG.
Telephone: 01938 555560
www.welshpoolairport.co.uk

WARWICKSHIRE
Almat Flying Club, Hanger 1, Coventry Airport, Bagington, Coventry,
Warwickshire CV8 3AZ.
Telephone: 0121 550 2644 E-mail: info@almat.co.uk
www.almat.co.uk

Atlantic Flight Training, Anson House, Coventry Airport, Coventry,
Warwickshire CV8 3AZ.
Telephone: 0845 450 0530 E-mail: enquiries@flyaft.com
www.atlanticflighttraining.com

Midland Air Training, Coventry Airport, Warwickshire CV3 4FR.
Telephone: 02476 304914 E-mail: info@mats.uki.net
www.midlandairtraining.uki.net

Pilot Flight Training, Wellesbourne Mountford Aerodrome, Wellesbourne,
Warwickshire CV35 9EU.
Telephone: 01789 470434
www.pftraining.co.uk

South Warwickshire Flying School, Wellesbourne Mountford Aerodrome,
Wellesbourne, Warwickshire CV35 9EU.
Telephone: 01789 840094
E-mail: principal@southwarwickshireflyingschool.com
www.southwarwickshireflyingschool.com

Take Flight Aviation, Wellesbourne Mountford Aerodrome, Wellesbourne, Warwickshire CV35 9EU.
Telephone: 01789 470424 E-mail: mike@takeflightaviation.co.uk
www.takeflightaviation.co.uk

Wellesbourne Aviation (Cabair), Wellesbourne Mountford Airfield, Wellesbourne, Warwickshire CV35 9EU.
Telephone: 01789 841066 E-mail: mail@wellaviate.co.uk
www.wellaviate.co.uk

WEST MIDLANDS
The Flying School, Building 29b, Wolverhampton Airport, Bobbington, Stourbridge, West Midlands DY7 5DY.
Telephone: 01384 221700
www.theflyingschoolltd.co.uk

Halfpenny Green Flight Centre, Wolverhampton Airport, Bobbington, Stourbridge, West Midlands DY7 5DY.
Telephone: 01384 221456 E-mail: operations@hgfc.co.uk
www.hgfc.co.uk

RJP Aviation, Wolverhampton Airport, Bobbington, Stourbridge, West Midlands DY7 5DY.
Telephone: 01384 221106 E-mail: rjpaviation@btconnect.com

WILTSHIRE
Abbas Air, Compton Abbas Airfield, Salisbury, Wiltshire SP5 5AP.
Telephone: 01747 811767 E-mail: fly@abbasair.com
www.abbasair.co.uk

Old Sarum Flying School, Hangar 3, Old Sarum Aerodrome, Portway, Salisbury, Wiltshire SP4 6DJ.
Telephone: 01722 322525 E-mail: info@oldsarumflyingclub.co.uk
www.oldsarumflyingclub.co.uk

YORKSHIRE – *see also* entries under **HUMBERSIDE**
Bagby Airfield Flying Club, Bagby Airfield, Bagby, North Yorkshire YD7 2PH.
Telephone: 01845 597385

Century Aviation, Sandtoft Aerodrome, Belton, Doncaster DN9 1PN.
Telephone: 07889 880985 E-mail: centuryavn@aol.com

Full Sutton Flying Centre, The Airfield, Full Sutton, York YO4 1HS.
Telephone: 01759 372717

Hull Aero Club, Linley Hill Airfield, Linley Hill Road, Leven, Beverley, North Humberside HU1Y 5LT.
Telephone: 01964 544994

Leeds Flying School, Sandtoft Aerodrome, Belton, Doncaster DN9 1PN.
Telephone: 01427 874875 E-mail: dylan@leedsflyingschool.com
www.leedsflyingschool.com

Multiflight, Leeds Bradford Airport, Yeadon, Leeds LS19 7UG.
Telephone: 0113 238 7130 E-mail: information@multiflight.co.uk
www.multiflight.co.uk

New Sandtoft Aviation, Sandtoft Aerodrome, Belton, Doncaster DN9 1PN.
Telephone: 01427 873676 E-mail: cfi@newsandtoftaviation.co.uk
www.newsandtoftaviation.co.uk

S & J Flight Training, Edds Field, Octon, Nr Langtoft, Driffield, East Yorkshire YO25 0BJ.
Telephone: 07930 279208

Sherburn Aero Club, The Aerodrome, Lennerton Lane, Sherburn-in-Elmet, Leeds LS25 6JE.
Telephone: 01977 682674 E-mail: flightdesk@sherburnaeroclub.com
www.sherburn-aero-club.org.uk

UK Private Pilot Licence Training Schools and Clubs – Helicopters

BEDFORDSHIRE

Cabair College of Air Training, Cranfield Airport, Cranfield, Bedfordshire MK43 0AL.
Telephone: 01234 751243 E-mail: beds@cabair.com
www.cabairflyingschools.com

Patriot Aviation, Hangar 1, Cranfield Airport, Cranfield, Bedfordshire MK43 0JR.
Telephone: 01234 752220 E-mail: training@patriot.uk.com
www.patriot.uk.com

BUCKINGHAMSHIRE

Heli Air, Wycombe Air Park, Marlow, Buckinghamshire SL7 3DP.
Telephone: 01494 451111
www.heliair.com

CAMBRIDGESHIRE

Cambridge Helicopters, The Helicentre, Cambridge Airport, Newmarket Road, Cambridgeshire CB5 8RX.
Telephone 01233 294488 E-mail: dbickley@aeromega.com
www.aeromega.com

M F H Helicopters, Erwin House, Peterborough Business Airfield, Holme Peterborough, Cambridgeshire PE7 3PX.
Telephone: 07779 086911
www.mfhhelicopters.co.uk

CHESHIRE

Hields Aviation, Hawarden Airport, Aviation Park, Flint Road, Saltney Ferry, Cheshire CH4 0GZ.
Telephone: 01244 537276 E-mail: fly@hieldsaviation.co.uk
www.hieldsaviation.co.uk

CORNWALL

Moorgoods Helicopters, Brake Farm, Penvorder Lane, St Breward, Bodmin, Cornwall PL30 4NY.
Telephone: 01208 850543
www.moorgoodshelicopters.co.uk

DEVON

Exeter Helicopters, 20 Grindle Way, Clyst St Mary, Exeter EX5 1DF.
Telephone: 01392 874508 E-mail: exeterhelicopters@hotmail.com

DORSET
Bournemouth Helicopters, Hangar 600, Bournemouth International Airport, Christchurch, Dorset BH23 6SE.
Telephone: 01202 590800 E-mail: info@bourne2fly.co.uk
www.bournemouth-helicopters.co.uk

ESSEX
AV8 Helicopters, Hangar 2, Aviation Way, London Southend Airport, Southend-on-Sea, Essex SS2 6VN.
Telephone: 01702 546354 E-mail: info@av8helicopters.co.uk
www.av8helicopters.co.uk

Helicentre Aviation, Damyns Hall Aerodrome, Aveley Road, Nr Hornchurch, Essex RM14 2TN.
Telephone: 01708 558696 E-mail: london@flyheli.co.uk
www.flyheli.co.uk

GLOUCESTERSHIRE
Astra Helicopters, The Flying Club, Kemble Airfield, Cirencester GL7 6BA.
Telephone: 01285 474727 E-mail: info@astrahelicopters.co.uk
www.astrahelicopters.co.uk

Cotswold Helicopters, The Old Fire Station, Kemble Airfield, Cirencester, Gloucestershire GL7 6BA.
Telephone: 01285 770740 E-mail: school@cotswoldhelicopters.co.uk
www.cotswoldhelicopters.co.uk

Heliflight, Gloucestershire Airport SE36, Cheltenham, Gloucestershire GL51 6SR.
Telephone: 01452 714555 E-mail: glosops@heliflightuk.co.uk
www.heliflightuk.com

Patriot Aviation, EC22 Gloucestershire Airport, Cheltenham, Gloucestershire GL51 6ST.
Telephone: 01452 859791 E-mail: candia.blenkiron@patriot.uk.com
www.patriot.uk.com

Proflight Helicopters, The Ground Floor Tower Building, Gloucestershire Airport, Cheltenham, Gloucestershire GL51 6SR.
Telephone: 01452 857177

HAMPSHIRE
Fast Helicopters, Hangar 2, Thruxton Airfield, Andover SP11 8PW.
Telephone: 01264 772508 E-mail: thruxton@fasthelicopters.com
www.fasthelicopters.com

HEREFORDSHIRE

Tiger Helicopters, Shobdon Airfield, Leominster HR6 9NR.
Telephone: 01568 708028 E-mail: alan@tigerhelicopters.co.uk
www.tigerhelicopters.co.uk

ISLE OF MAN

Helimanx, Croite Orry, Main Road, Kirk Michael, Isle of Man IM6 1AJ.
Telephone: 01624 877770 E-mail: info@helimanx.com
www.helimanx.com

KENT

AV8 Helicopters, The Heliport, Rochester Airport, Maidstone Road,
Chatham, Kent ME5 9SD.
Telephone: 01634 672288 E-mail: info@av8helicopters.co.uk
www.av8helicopters.co.uk

Biggin Hill Helicopters, Hangar 500, Biggin Hill Airport, Westerham, Kent
TN16 3BN.
Telephone: 01959 540803 E-mail: enquiry@bhh.co.uk
www.bhh.co.uk

Thurston Helicopters, Headcorn Aerodrome, Headcorn TN27 9HX.
Telephone: 01622 891158 E-mail: mail@thurstonhelis.co.uk
www.thurstonhelis.co.uk

LANCASHIRE

D C Aviation, Hangar 3, Blackpool Airport, Blackpool FY4 2QY.
Telephone: 01253 407070

Heli 2000, Blackpool Airport, Blackpool FY4 2QY.
Telephone: 01253 298802 E-mail: heli2000_blackpool@yahoo.co.uk
www.heli2000.co.uk

Helicentre Blackpool, Blackpool Airport, Blackpool FY4 2QY.
Telephone: 01253 343082 E-mail: blackpool@helicentre.com
www.helicentreblackpool.com

Heli North West, Barton Aerodrome, Eccles, Lancashire M30 7SA.
Telephone: 07745 012695 E-mail: gary@heli-nw.co.uk
www.heli-nw.co.uk

The Manchester Helicopter Centre, Barton Aerodrome, Eccles,
Lancashire M30 7SA.
Telephone: 0161 787 7125
www.themanchesterhelicoptercentre.co.uk

LEICESTERSHIRE

HeliEagle, Leicester Airport, Gartree Road, Leicester LE2 2FG.
Telephone: 0116 259 0010 E-mail: sales@helieagle.com
www.helieagle.com

MERSEYSIDE

Helicentre, Business Aviation Centre, Viscount Drive, Liverpool Airport,
Liverpool L24 5GA.
Telephone: 0151 448 0388 E-mail: liverpool@helicentre.com
www.helicentre.com

MIDDLESEX

Heli Air, Hangar Road, Denham Aerodrome, Uxbridge UB9 5DF.
Telephone: 01895 835899
www.heliair.com

NORFOLK

Anglian Helicopters, Hangar 12, Gambling Close, Norwich Airport,
Norwich NR6 6EG.
Telephone: 01603 410866

Broad Air Services, Old School House, Lingwood, Norwich NR13 4TJ.
Telephone: 01603 712570 E-mail: npbroad@yahoo.co.uk

Sterling Aviation, Hangar E, Gambling Close, Norwich Airport, Norwich
NR6 6EG.
Telephone: 01603 417156 E-mail: info@flysterling.com
www.flysterling.com

NORTHAMPTONSHIRE

Sloane Helicopters, The Business Aviation Centre, Sywell Aerodrome,
Northampton NN6 0BN.
Telephone: 01604 790595 E-mail: training@sloanehelicopters.com
www.sloanehelicopters.co.uk

NORTHERN IRELAND

Helicopter Training & Hire, The Helicopter Centre, Newtownards Airfield,
28 Comber Road, Newtownards, County Down, Northern Ireland BT23
4QP.
Telephone: 028 918 20028 E-mail: info@helicoptercentre.co.uk
www.helicoptercentre.co.uk

Shoreham Helicopters, Enniskillen Airport, Trory, County Fermanagh,
Northern Ireland BT94 2FP.
Telephone: 07739 403247

Unique Helicopters, Enniskillen Airport, Ballinamallard, County Fermanagh, Northern Ireland BT94 2FP.
Telephone: 02866 326636 E-mail: uniqueheli@yahoo.com
www.uniquehelicopters.co.uk

NORTHUMBERLAND
Northumbria Helicopters, Newcastle International Airport, Southside, Woolsington, Newcastle -upon-Tyne, Northumberland NE13 8BT.
Telephone: 0191 271 5999 E-mail: nhl@northumbria-helicopters.co.uk
www.northumbria-helicopters.co.uk

NOTTINGHAMSHIRE
Central Helicopters, Nottingham Airport, Tollerton Lane, Tollerton, Nottinghamshire NG12 4GA.
Telephone: 01159 814401 E-mail: info@centralhelicopters.com
www.centralhelicopters.com

SCOTLAND
Helicentre Liverpool, Fife (Glenrothes) Airport, Goatmilk, Glenrothes, Fife KY6 2SL.
Telephone: 07919 276592 E-mail: Liverpool@helicentre.com
www.helicentre.com

Helijaf, Leading Edge Flight Training, Cumbernauld Airport, Duncan McIntosh Road, Cumbernauld, Glasgow G68 0HH.
Telephone: 01236 727272 E-mail: jfairley34@yahoo.com

HJS Helicopters, Culter Helipad, Lower Baads, Anguston, Peterculter, Aberdeenshire AB14 0PR.
Telephone: 0870 850 3313 E-mail: information@hjshelicopters.co.uk
www.hjshelicopters.co.uk

Kingsfield Helicopters, Scottish Aeroclub Building, Perth Airport, Perth & Kinross PH2 6PL.
Telephone: 01738 554851 E-mail: info@kingsfield-helicopters.co.uk
www.kingsfield-helicopters.co.uk

Mach Aviation, Comet House, Building 97, Business Area, Edinburgh Airport, Edinburgh EH12 9DN.
Telephone: 07939 138078 E-mail: mail@machaviation.co.uk
www.machaviation.co.uk

Mach Aviation, Fife (Glenrothes) Airport, Goatmilk, Glenrothes KY6 2SL.
Telephone: 07939 138078 E-mail: mail@machaviation.co.uk
www.machaviation.co.uk

Scotia Helicopters, Duncan McIntosh Road, Cumbernauld, Glasgow G68 0HH.
Telephone: 01236 780140 E-mail: info@scotiahelicopters.co.uk
www.scotiahelicopters.co.uk

SOMERSET
Bristol Helicopters, The Hangars, Bristol International Airport, Bristol, Somerset BS48 3EP.
Telephone: 01275 474727 E-mail: info@astrahelicopters.co.uk
www.astrahelicopters.co.uk

Rotorflight, Bristol Flying Centre, Bristol International Airport, Bristol, Somerset BS34 3DP.
Telephone: 07831 146455 E-mail: paulchapman@rotorflight.co.uk
www.rotorflight.co.uk

STAFFORDSHIRE
Heliflight, Wolverhampton Business Airport, Bobbington, Stourbridge, Staffordshire DY7 5DY.
Telephone: 01384 221215 E-mail: wba@heliflightuk.co.uk
www.heliflightuk.com

Staffordshire Helicopters, Tatenhill Airfield, Newborough Road, Needwood, Burton-upon-Trent, Staffordshire DE13 9PD.
Telephone: 01283 575283 E-mail: info@staffordshirehelicopters.com
www.staffordshirehelicopters.com

SUFFOLK
Egan Helicopters, 37 Beccles Road, Oulton Broad, Lowestoft, Suffolk NR33 8QT.
Telephone: 01502 582076

Forfly Helicopter Services, Beccles Airfield, Beccles, Suffolk LN34 7TE.
Telephone: 01986 788410 E-mail: forflyhelicopters@ntlworld.com

SURREY
DNH Helicopters, Hangar 6, Redhill Aerodrome, Redhill, Surrey RH1 5JY.
Telephone: 01737 822915 E-mail: info@dnhhelicopters.co.uk
www.dnhhelicopters.co.uk

Alan Mann Helicopters, Fairoaks Airport, Chobham, Woking, Surrey GU24 8HX.
Telephone: 01276 857471 E-mail: helitraining@alanmann.co.uk
www.alanmann.co.uk

Redhill Helicopter Centre, Hangar 1, Redhill Aerodrome, Redhill, Surrey RH1 5JY.
Telephone: 01737 823282 E-mail: mail@ebghelicopters.co.uk
www.ebghelicopters.co.uk

SUSSEX
Elite Helicopters and Aviation Services, Hangar 3, Goodwood Airfield, Chichester, West Sussex PO18 0PH.
Telephone: 0800 804 8812 E-mail: ops@elitehelicopters.co.uk
www.elitehelicopters.co.uk

Fast Helicopters, Shoreham Airport, Shoreham-by-Sea BN43 5FF.
Telephone: 01273 465389 E-mail: shoreham@fasthelicopters.com
www.fashhelicopters.com

Shoreham Helicopters, 4 Highdown House, Shoreham Airport, Shoreham-by-Sea BN43 5FF.
Telephone: 07739 403247 E-mail: tim.price@talk21.com

WALES
Heli-air Wales, Swansea Airport, Swansea, West Glamorgan SA2 7JU.
Telephone: 01792 202250
www.heli-airwales.co.uk

Proflight Helicopters, Pembrey Airport, Pembrey SA16 0HZ.
Telephone: 07836 265004

Proflight Helicopters, Swansea Airport, Swansea, West Glamorgan SA2 7JU.
Telephone: 07836 265004

Whizzard Helicopters, Mid-Wales Airport, Welshpool, Powys SY21 8SG.
Telephone: 01938 55860 E-mail: info@whizzardhelicopters.co.uk
www.whizzardhelicopters.co.uk

WARWICKSHIRE
Flight Training, Coventry Airport, Rowley Road, Coventry, Warwickshire CV3 4FR.
Telephone: 02476 639625 E-mail: info@heli.org
www.heli.org

Heli Air, Wellesbourne Airfield, Wellesbourne Mountford, Warwickshire CV35 9EU.
Telephone: 01789 470476
www.heliair.com

Helicentre Aviation, Anson House, Baginton, Coventry Airport West, Warwickshire CV8 3AZ.
Telephone: 02476 511615 E-mail: info@flyheli.co.uk
www.flyheli.co.uk

YORKSHIRE
Alpha Helicopters, Sheffield City Airport, Europa Link, Sheffield S9 1XZ.
Telephone: 0870 708 1111 E-mail: info@helicopters.co.uk
www.helicopters.co.uk

Dragon Helicopters, Sheffield City Airport, Europa Link, Sheffield S9 1XZ.
Telephone: 0114 201 5425 E-mail: info@dragonhelicopters.co.uk
www.dragonhelicopters.co.uk

Hields Aviation, Sherburn Airfield, Lennerton Lane, Sherburn-in-Elmet, Leeds LS25 6JE.
Telephone: 01977 680206 E-mail: fly@hieldsaviation.co.uk
www.hieldsaviation.co.uk

Sandtoft Helicopters, Sandtoft Aerodrome, Sandtoft, Belton, Doncaster, South Yorkshire DN9 1PN.
Telephone: 01427 874949 E-mail: fly@hclicoptcrs.co.uk
www.helicopterfly.co.uk

Professional Pilot Flight Training Schools – UK

Atlantic Flight Training,** Coventry Airport, Coventry, CV8 3AZ.
Telephone: 0845 450 0530 E-mail: enquiries@flyaft.com
www.atlanticflighttraining.com

Bournemouth Commercial Flight Training Centre,** Building 33, Red
Zone, Bournemouth International Airport, Christchurch BH23 6ED.
Telephone: 01202 599888 E-mail: lance.plews@bcft.org.uk
www.bcft.org.uk

Bristol Ground School,** Lower New Road, Cheddar BS27 3DY.
Telephone: 01934 744944 E-mail: info@bristol.gs
www.bristol.gs

Cabair College of Air Training, Cranfield Aerodrome, Cranfield, Bedford,
Bedfordshire MK43 0JR.
Telephone: 01234 751243 E-mail: cranfield@cabair.com
www.cabair.com

Cranfield Aviation Training School,** Building 175, Cranfield Airport,
Cranfield, Bedfordshire MK43 0JR.
Telephone: 01234 757969 E-mail: info@cranfieldaviation.co.uk
www.cranfieldaviation.co.uk

CTC Aviation Training, Discovery Centre, Eastern Business Park,
Bournemouth International Airport, Christchurch, Dorset BH23 6DD.
Telephone: 01202 331540
www.ctcaviation.com

Ground Training Services,** Building 66, SE Sector, Bournemouth
International Airport, Christchurch, Dorset BH23 6SE.
Telephone: 01202 580809 E-mail: roger@gtserv.co.uk
www.gtserv.co.uk

Oxford Aviation Training, Oxford Airport, Kidlington OX5 1QX.
Telephone: 01865 841234 E-mail: oatsmktg@oxfordaviation.net
www.oxfordaviation.net

London Metropolitan University,** Centre for Civil Aviation, 100
Minories, London EC3N 1JY.
Telephone: 020 7320 1757 E-mail: aviation@londonmet.ac.uk
www.londonmet.ac.uk

**Ground tuition only. These establishments do not offer flying training.

CAA Approved Overseas Flight Training Schools

The following organizations have been authorized by the CAA to conduct training for various pilot licences and ratings to the JAR-FCL syllabuses. Potential students are recommended to satisfy themselves as to the full details of any course and ground school exams before committing to training.

Fixed-wing

Anglo American Aviation, 2035 North Marshall Avenue, El Cajon, San Diego, California 92020, USA.
Telephone: 001 619 448 9149 E-mail: info@flyaaa.com
www.flyaaa.com

European Flight Training, 3800 St Lucie Boulevard, Fort Pierce, Florida 34946, USA.
Telephone: 001 772 466 4757 E-mail: info@flyeft.com
www.flyeft.com

Flight Training Europe, Aeropuerto de Jerez, Antigua Base Militar 'La Parra', 11400 Jerez de la Frontera, Cadiz, Spain.
Telephone: 0034 956 317800 E-mail:
cristina.vazquez@flighttrainingeurope.com
www.flighttrainingeurope.com

Naples Air Center, 230 Aviation Drive South, Naples, Florida 34104, USA.
Telephone : 001 239 643 1717 E-mail: admissions@naples-air-center.com
www.naples-air-center.com

Ormond Beach Aviation, Ormond Beach Municipal Airport, 770 Airport Road, Suite 7, Ormond Beach, Florida 32174 USA.
Telephone: 001 386 673 2899 E-mail: info@flyoba.com
www.flyoba.com

Western Australian Aviation College, 41 Eagle Drive, Jandakot Airport, Western Australia 6164.
Telephone: 0061 8 9417 7733
E-mail: craigpeterson@waaviationcollege.com.au
www.waaviationcollege.com.au

Helicopter

Bristow Academy, Space Coast Regional Airport, 3265 Golden Knights Boulevard, Titusville, Florida 32780, USA.
Telephone: 001 321 385 2919 E-mail: info@heli.com
www.heli.com

British Airlines, Scheduled, Charter and Cargo Operators

Air Atlantique, Dakota House, Coventry Airport, Warwickshire
CV8 3AZ.
Telephone: 02476 882630 E-mail: operations@atlanticairlines.co.uk
www.atlanticairlines.co.uk

Air Charter Scotland, 7 Colvilles Place, Kelvin Industrial Estate, East
Kilbride, Glasgow G75 0PZ.
Telephone: 01355 590300 E-mail: info@aircharterscotland.com
www.aircharterscotland.com

Air Kilroe, Room 15, Level 7, Terminal One, Manchester International
Airport, Manchester M90 3AL.
Telephone: 0161 436 2055 E-mail: info@easternairways.com
www.easternairways.com

Air Partner Private Jets, Platinum House, Gatwick Road, Crawley
RH10 9RP.
Telephone: 01293 844800
www.airpartner.com

Air Southwest, Plymouth City Airport, Crownhill, Plymouth PL6 8BW.
Telephone: 0870 043 4553 E-mail: recruitment@airsouthwest.com
www.airsouthwest.com

Astraeus, Astraeus House, Faraday Court, Faraday Road, Crawley, West
Sussex RH10 9PU.
www.flystar.com

Atlantic Airlines – *see* entry under **Air Atlantique**

Aurigny Air Services, States Airport, La Planque Lane, Forest, Guernsey,
Channel Islands GY8 0TD.
Telephone: 01481 266444
www.aurigny.com

BAC Express Airlines, 2morrow Court, Appleford Road, Sutton Courtenay,
Oxon OX14 4FH.
Telephone: 01235 844150 E-mail: mail@bacexpress.com
www.bacexpress.com

Blue Islands, St Peter Port, Guernsey, Channel Islands.
Telephone: 01481 711321 E-mail: jobs@blueislands.com
www.blueislands.com

Bond Air Services, Gloucestershire Airport, Staverton, Cheltenham, Gloucestershire GL51 6SP.
Telephone: 01452 856007 E-mail: info@bondairservices.com
www.bondairservices.com

Bristow Helicopters, Redhill Aerodrome, Redhill, Surrey RH1 5JZ.
 Telephone: 01737 822353
www.bristowgroup.com

British Airways, Waterside, PO Box 365, Harmondsworth, UB7 0GB.
Telephone: 0870 608 0747 E-mail: BARecruitment@ba.com
www.ba.com

British International, Coldharbour Business Park, Sherborne, Dorset DT9 4JW.
Telephone: 01935 389425
www.islesofscillyhelicopter.com

British Midland (BMI), Donington Hall, Castle Donington, Derbyshire DE74 2SB.
Telephone: 01332 854000
www.flybmi.com

Club 328, Hangar 2, Southampton International Airport, Hampshire SO18 2HG.
Telephone: 01273 248800
www.club328.com

DHL Air, East Midlands Airport, Castle Donington, Derby DE74 2TR.
Telephone: 01332 857815
www.dhl.co.uk

Direct Flight, Building 84A, Cranfield Airport, Cranfield, Bedfordshire MK43 0AL.
Telephone: 01234 757766 E-mail: cfd.hq@directflight.co.uk
www.directflight.co.uk

Easyjet, Hangar 89, London Luton Airport, Bedfordshire LU2 9PF.
E-mail: flightcrew.recruitment@easyjet.com
www.easyjet.com

Eurojet Aviation, Old Terminal Area, NCP Building, Birmingham International Airport, Birmingham B26 3QJ.
Telephone: 0121 782 1700 E-mail: enquiries@eurojet.eu.com
www.eurojet.eu.com

European Air Charter, European Aviation House, Bournemouth International Airport, Christchurch, Dorset BH23 6EA.
Telephone: 01202 581111
www.eaac.co.uk

European Business Jets, Aviation House, The Exchange, Station Road, Stansted CM24 8BE.
Telephone: 01279 817464 E-mail: info@europeanbusinessjets.com
www.europeanbusinessjets.com

Executive Jet Charter, Business Aviation Centre, Farnborough Airport, Farnborough, Hampshire GU14 6XA.
Telephone: 01242 244088 E-mail: info@execjet.co.uk
www.execjet.co.uk

First Choice Airways, Commonwealth House, Chicago Avenue, Manchester Airport, Manchester M90 3DP.
Telephone: 0161 489 0325 E-mail: kerry.fox@firstchoice.co.uk
www.firstchoice.co.uk

FlightLine, Viscount House, Southend Airport, Southend-on-Sea SS2 6YF.
Telephone: 01702 543000 E-mail: enquiries@flightline.ltd.uk
www.flightline.ltd.uk

Flybe, Jack Walker House, Exeter International Airport, Exeter EX5 2HL.
E-mail: pilots.personnel@flybe.com
www.flybe.com

FR Aviation, Bournemouth International Airport, Christchurch BH23 6NE.
Telephone: 01202 409000
www.fraviation.com

Gama Aviation, Business Aviation Centre, Farnborough Airport, Hampshire GU14 6XA.
Telephone: 01252 553000 E-mail: operations@gamagroup.com
www.gamagroup.com

GB Airways, The Beehive, Beehive Ring Road, Gatwick Airport, West Sussex RH6 0LA.
Telephone: 01293 664239
www.gbairways.com

Global Supply Systems, Stansted House, Stansted Airport CM24 1AE.
Telephone: 01279 682900 E-mail: admin@gssair.co.uk
www.gssair.co.uk

Globespan Airways, Atlantic House, 38 Gardners Crescent, Edinburgh EH3 8DQ.
www.flyglobespan.com

Hebridean Air Services, Cumbernauld Airport, Glasgow G68 0HH.
Telephone: 01236 457777 E-mail: info@hebrideanair.com

Highland Airways, Kerrowgair House, Inverness Airport, Inverness IV2 7QU.
Telephone: 01667 462664 E-mail: info@highlandairways.co.uk
www.highlandairways.co.uk

Interflight, Hangar 503, Churchill Way, Biggin Hill Airport, Westerham, Kent TN16 3BN.
Telephone: 01959 575800 E-mail: info@interflight.co.uk
www.interflight.co.uk

Isles of Scilly Skybus, Quay Street, Penzance, Cornwall TR18 4BZ.
Telephone: 01736 334220
www.islesofscilly-travel.co.uk

Jet2.com, Low Fare Finder House, Leeds Bradford International Airport, Leeds LS19 7TU.
www.jet2.com

Jet Options, Elmdon Terminal Building, Birmingham International Airport, Birmingham B26 3QN.
Telephone: 0121 782 1011 E-mail: mail@jet-options.com
www.jet-options.com

Jetstream Executive Travel, 18 Rumer Hill Business Estate, Rumer Hill Road, Cannock, Staffordshire WS11 0ET.
Telephone: 01543 469924 E-mail: info@jetstreamexec.co.uk
www.jetstreamexec.co.uk

Loganair, St Andrews Drive, Glasgow Airport, Paisley, Scotland PA3 2TG.
Telephone: 0141 848 7594
www.loganair.co.uk

London Executive Aviation, London City Airport, Royal Docks, London E16 2PX.
Telephone: 020 7474 3344
www.flylea.com

Lydd Air, Lydd Airport, Lydd, Romney Marsh, Kent TN29 9QL.
E-mail: enquiries@lyddair.com
www.lyddair.com

Manhattan Jet Charter, Business Aviation Centre, Farnborough
International Airport, Farnborough, Hampshire GU14 6XA.
Telephone: 01252 375500
www.manhattanjetcharter.com

Markoss Aviation, Jet Centre Hangar 527, Biggin Hill Airport, Westerham,
Kent TN16 3BN.
Telephone: 01959 570559
www.markoss-aviation.com

MAS Airways, First Floor, 67 Victoria Road, Horley, Surrey RH6 7QH.
Telephone: 01293 825197 E-mail: rl@masairways.com
www.masairways.com

MK Airlines, Landhurst, Hartfield, East Sussex TN7 4DH.
Telephone: 01892 770011
www.mkairlines.com

Monarch Airlines, Prospect House, Prospect Way, Luton International
Airport, Bedfordshire LU2 9NU.
Telephone: 01582 398364
www.flymonarch.com

Silverjet Aviation, 72/104 Frank Lester Way, London Luton Airport,
Bedfordshire LU2 9NQ.
0844 855 0111 E-mail: pleasehireme@flysilverjet.com
www.flysilverjet.com

ScotAirways, Cambridge Airport, Cambridge CB5 8RT
Telephone: 01223 378328
www.scotairways.com

Thomas Cook Airlines, Commonwealth House, Chicago Avenue,
Manchester Airport, Manchester M90 3FL.
E-mail: pilotrecruitment@thomascook.com
www.thomascookairlines.co.uk

ThomsonFly, Columbus House, Westwood Way, Westwood Business Park,
Coventry CV4 8TT.
E-mail: webjobs@uk.britanniaaways.com
www.thomsonfly.com

Titan Airways, Enterprise House, Stansted Airport, Stansted, Essex CM24 1RN.
Telephone: 01279 680616
www.titan-airways.com

Twinjet Aircraft Sales, Essex House, Proctor Way, London Luton Airport, Luton, Bedfordshire LU2 9PE.
Telephone: 01582 452888 E-mail: recruitment@twinjet.co.uk
www.twinjet.co.uk

UK International Airlines, 308–318 Queens Road, Sheffield S2 4DL.
Telephone: 0870 990 9027 E-mail: recruitment@ukinternationalairlines.com
www.ukinternationalairlines.com

Virgin Atlantic Airways, The Office, Manor Royal, Crawley, West Sussex RH10 9NU.
Telephone: 01293 562345 E-mail: recruitment.services@fly.virgin.com
www.fly.virgin.com

XClusive Jet Charter, International House, Southampton International Airport, Southampton, Hampshire SO18 2RX.
Telephone: 02380 696992
www.exclusivejet.com

XL Airways, Explorer House, Fleming Way, Crawley, West Sussex, RH10 9EA.
www.excelairways.com

Zoom Airlines, First Floor, Iain Stewart Centre, Beehive Ring Road, City Place, Gatwick Airport, West Sussex RH6 0PB.
E-mail: UKFlightCrewJobs@flyzoom.com
www.flyzoom.com

Contact Addresses – Private, Commercial and Airline Pilots

International Council of Aircraft Owner & Pilot Associations (IAOPA), 421 Aviation Way, Frederick, MD 21701, USA
Telephone: 001 301 695 2220 Email: airmail@iaopa.org
www.iaopa.org

Aircraft Owners & Pilots Association (UK), 50a Cambridge Street, London SW1V 4QQ.
Telephone: 0207 834 5631 Email: info@aopa.co.uk
www.aopa.co.uk

Aircraft Owners & Pilots Association (USA), 421 Aviation Way, Frederick, Maryland 21701, USA
Telephone: 001 301 695 2000 Email: aopahq@aopa.org
www.aopa.org

British Air Line Pilots Association, BALPA House, 5 Heathrow Boulevard, 278 Bath Road, West Drayton, UB7 0DQ.
Telephone: 0208 476 4000 Email: balpa@balpa.org
www.balpa.org.uk

British Helicopter Advisory Board, The Graham Suite, West Entrance, Fairoaks Airport, Chobham, Surrey GU24 8HX.
Telephone: 01276 856100 Email: info@bhab.org
www.bhab.flyer.co.uk

Civil Aviation Authority (flight crew licensing), Personnel Licensing Department, Aviation House, Gatwick Airport, West Sussex RH6 0YR.
Telephone: 01293 573700
www.caa.co.uk

Civil Aviation Authority (medical), Medical Department, Aviation House, Gatwick Airport South, West Sussex RH6 0YR.
Telephone: 01293 573685
www.caa.co.uk

Guild of Air Pilots & Air Navigators, Cobham House, 9 Warwick Court, Gray's Inn, London WC1R 5DJ.
Telephone: 0207 404 4032 Email; gapan@gapan.org
www.gapan.org

PPL/IR Europe, The Business Centre, Llangarron, Ross-on-Wye HR9 6PG.
E-mail: memsec@pplir.org
www.pplir.org

Contact Addresses – Military

Royal Air Force
If you require more details of an RAF career, visit the RAF web site, telephone the careers enquiry number given below or visit one of the Armed Forces Careers Offices on the following list.
Telephone: 0845 605 5555
www.raf.mod.uk/careers

Air Cadets and Air Training Corps
Headquarters Air Cadets, RAF Cranwell, Sleaford, Lincolnshire NG34 8HB.
Telephone: (switchboard) 01400 261201
www.aircadets.org

University Air Squadrons
RAF Cranwell, Sleaford, Lincolnshire NG34 8HB.
Telephone: (switchboard) 01400 261201.
www.universityairsquadrons.com

Royal Navy
If you require more details of a Royal Navy career, visit the Royal Navy web site, telephone the careers enquiry number given below or visit one of the Armed Forces Career Offices on the following list.
Telephone: 0845 607 5555
www.careers.royalnavy.mod.uk/careers

British Army
If you require more details of an Army career, visit the Army web site, telephone the career enquiry number given below or visit one of the Armed Forces Career Offices on the following list.
Telephone: 0845 300 111
www.armyjobs.mod.uk

Armed Forces Careers Offices
Aberdeen – 63 Belmont Street, AB10 1JS.
Belfast – Palace Barracks, Holywood, BT18 9RA.
Birmingham – 46 The Pallasades, B2 4XN.
Bournemouth – 244 Holdenhurst Road, BH8 8AZ.
Brighton – 120–121 Queens Road, BN1 3WB.
Bristol – 4 Colston Avenue, BS1 4TZ.
Cambridge – Bateman House, 82-88 Hills Road, CB2 1LQ.
Canterbury – 17 St Peter's Street, CT1 2BQ.
Cardiff – Southgate House, Wood Street, CF10 1GR.
Carlisle – 94–96 English Street, CA3 8ND.
Chatham – 3 Dock Road, ME4 4SJ.

Chelmsford – 1/3 Dorset House, Duke Street, CM1 1HQ.
Coventry – 60 Hertford Street, CV1 1LB.
Darlington – 148 Northgate, DL1 1QT.
Derby – 3rd Floor, Sitwell House, Sitwell Street, DE1 2JT.
Dundee – 29–31 Bank Street, DD1 1RW.
Edinburgh – 67–83 Shandwick Place, EH2 4SN.
Exeter – Fountain House, Western Way, EX1 2DQ.
Glasgow – Charlotte House, 78 Queen Street, G1 3DN.
Gloucester – Britannia Warehouse, The Docks, GL1 2EH.
Guildford – Stamford House, 91 Woodbridge Road, GU1 4QE.
Hull – Norwich House, Savile Street, HU1 3ES.
Ilford – 180a Cranbrook Road, IG1 4LR.
Inverness – 3 Bridge Street, IV1 1HG.
Ipswich – 37 Silent Street, IP1 1TF.
Leeds – 10–14 Bond Court, LS1 2JY.
Leicester – St George's House, 6 St George's Way, LE1 1SH.
Lincoln – Sibthorpe House, 350–352 High Street, LN5 7BN.
Liverpool – Victoria House, 15 James Street, L2 7NX.
London – St George's Court, 2–12 Bloomsbury Way, WC1A 2SH.
Luton – Dunstable House, Dunstable Road, LU1 1EA.
Manchester – Petersfield House, 29–31 Peter Street, M2 5QJ.
Middlesbrough – 69 Borough Road, TS1 3AD.
Newcastle-upon-Tyne – 10 Ridley Place, NE1 8JW.
Norwich – 22 Unthank Road, NR2 2RA.
Nottingham – 70 Victoria Centre, Milton Street, NG1 3QX.
Oxford – 35 St Giles, OX1 3LJ.
Peterborough – 23 Hereward Centre, PE1 1TB.
Plymouth – Pilgrim House, Derry's Cross, PL1 2SW.
Portsmouth – Cambridge Road, PO1 2EN.
Preston – 83a Fishergate, PR1 2NJ.
Reading – 19–20 St Mary's Butts, RG1 2LN.
Redruth – Oak House, Chapel Street, TR15 2BY.
St Helens – 63 College Street, Merseyside, WA10 1TN.
Sheffield – Central Buildings, 1a Church Street, S1 2GJ.
Shrewsbury – 2nd Floor, Princess House, The Square, SY1 1JZ.
Southampton – 152 High Street, Below Bar, SO14 2BT.
Southend-on-Sea – Level 3 Chartwell Square, Victoria Plaza, SS2 5SP.
Stoke-on-Trent – 36–38 Old Hall Street, Hanley, ST1 3AP.
Swansea – 17–19 Castle Street, SA1 1JF.
Taunton – 35 East Street, TA1 3LS.
Wolverhampton – 43a Queen Street, WV1 3BL.
Wrexham – 21 Rhosddu Road, LL1 1NE.

Pilot Publications and Equipment Retailers

Aeronautical Information Service, NATS Ltd, Control Tower Building, London Heathrow Airport, Hounslow, Middlesex TW6 1JJ.
Telephone: 0208 745 3456 Email: ais.supervisor@nats.co.uk
www.ais.org.uk

Airlife Publishing, The Crowood Press Ltd, Ramsbury, Marlborough, Wiltshire, SN8 2HR.
Telephone: 01672 520320 Email: enquiries@crowood.com
www.crowood.com

CAA documents – The Stationery Office, PO Box 29, St Crispins House, Duke Street, Norwich NR3 1GN.
Telephone: 0870 600 5522 E-mail: customer.services@tso.co.uk
www.clicktso.com

Flight International magazine (weekly), Quadrant House, The Quadrant, Sutton, Surrey SM2 5AS.
www.flightinternational.com

Flyer magazine (monthly), Seager Publishing, 9 Riverside Court, Lower Bristol Road, Bath, BA2 3DZ
Telephone: 01225 481440
www.flyer.co.uk

Harry Mendelssohn Discount Sales, 49–51 Colinton Road, Edinburgh EH10 5DH.
Telephone: 0131 447 7777 Email: sales@gps.co.uk
www.gps.co.uk

JAA documents – RAPIDOC (and Technical Indexes Ltd), Willoughby Road, Bracknell, Berkshire RG12 8DW.
Telephone: 01344 426311 Email: rapidoc@techindex.co.uk
www.techindex.co.uk/rapidoc

LOOP newspaper (monthly – free), LOOP Publishing UK Ltd, 9–11 The Mill Courtyard, Copley Hill Business Park, Cambridge CB22 3GN
Telephone: 01223 497060
www.loop.aero

Pilot magazine (monthly), Archant Specialist, The Mill, Bearwalden Business Park, Wendens Ambo, Essex, CB11 4GB.
Telephone: 01799 544200
www.pilotweb.aero

Pooley's Flight Equipment Ltd, Elstree Aerodrome, Elstree, Hertfordshire WD6 3AW.
Telephone: 0208 207 3749 Email: sales@pooleys.com
www.pooleys.com

Airplan Flight Equipment Ltd, (Shop) Oxford Airport, Kidlington, Oxford OX5 1QX; (Mail order) 1a Ringway Trading Estate, Shadowmoss Road, Manchester, M22 5LH.
Telephone: (Shop) 01865 841 441; (Mail order) 0161 499 0023 Fax: (Shop) 01865 842 495; (Mail order) 0161 499 0298
Email: (Shop) tech@afeonline.com; (Mail order) afe@afeonline.com
www.afeonline.com

Today's Pilot magazine (monthly), Key Publishing, PO Box 100, Stamford, Lincolnshire, PE9 1XQ.
Telephone: 01780 755131
www.todayspilot.co.uk

Transair Pilot Shops:
Shoreham Airport, Shoreham-by-sea, West Sussex, BN43 5PA
Telephone: (Shop) 01273 466018; (Mail order) 01273 466000
Email: info@transair.co.uk
Fairoaks Airport, Chobham, Surrey GU24 8HU.
Telephone: 01276 855962
50a Cambridge Street, London SW1V 4QQ.
Telephone: 0207 976 6787
1st Floor, Aviation House, Gloucestershire Airport, Staverton, Cheltenham, GL51 6SR.
Telephone: 01452 856749
www.transair.co.uk

Contact Addresses – Aviation Related

British Aerobatic Association Ltd, c/o West London Aero Club, White Waltham Airfield, Maidenhead, Berkshire SL6 3NJ.
Telephone: 01487 833022   Email: membership@aerobatics.org.uk
www.aerobatics.org.uk

British Balloon and Airship Club, St John's Street, Bedminster, Bristol, BS3 4NH.
Telephone: 0117 953 1231   Email: information@bbac.org
www.bbac.org

British Business and General Aviation Association, 19 Church Street, Brill, Aylesbury, Buckinghamshire HP18 9RT.
Telephone: 01844 238 020   Email: info@bbga.aero
www.bbga.aero

British Disabled Flying Association, c/o Lasham Gliding Society, Lasham Airfield, Alton, Hampshire, GU34 5SS.
Telephone: 07967 269 345   Email: info@bdfa.net
www.bdfa.net

British Gliding Association, Kimberley House, Vaughan Way, Leicester LE1 4SE.
Telephone: 0116 253 1051   Email: office@gliding.co.uk
www.gliding.co.uk

British Hang Gliding & Paragliding Association, The Old Schoolroom, Loughborough Road, Leicester LE4 5PJ.
Telephone: 0116 261 1322   Email: office@bhpa.co.uk
www.bhpa.co.uk

British Microlight Aircraft Association, The Bullring, Deddington, Oxfordshire OX15 0TT.
Telephone: 01869 338 888   Email: general@bmaa.org
www.bmaa.org

British Parachute Association, 5 Wharf Way, Glen Parva, Leicester LE2 9TF.
Telephone: 0116 2785 271   Email: skydive@bpa.org.uk
www.bpa.org.uk

British Women Pilots Association, c/o Brooklands Museum, Brooklands Road, Weybridge, Surrey, KT13 0QN.
Email: info@bwpa.co.uk
www.bwpa.co.uk

General Aviation Awareness Council, RAeS House, 4 Hamilton Place, London, W1J 7BQ.
Telephone: 0207 670 4501 Email: info@gaac.org.uk
www.gaac.co.uk

General Aviation Safety Council, Rochester Airport, Chatham, Kent, ME5 9SD.
Telephone: 01634 200203 Email: info@gasco.org.uk
www.gasco.org.uk

Helicopter Club of Great Britain, Ryelands House, Aynho, Banbury, Oxfordshire OX17 3AT.
Email: jeremy@ryelands.net
www.hcgb.co.uk

International Air Tattoo Flying Scholarships for the Disabled, Douglas Bader House, Horcott Hill, Fairford, Gloucestershire, GL7 4RB.
Telephone: 0870 800 1942 Email: info@toreachforthesky.org.uk
www.toreachforthesky.org.uk

Light Aircraft Association, Turweston Aerodrome, Brackley, Northamptonshire, NN13 5YD.
Telephone: 01280 846786 Email: office@laa.uk.com
www.laa.uk.com

National Pilot's Licensing Group (NPLG), Turweston Aerodrome, Nr Brackley, Northamptonshire NN13 5YD.
Telephone: 01280 846786
www.nppl.uk.com

Royal Aero Club, Kimberley House, Vaughan Way, Leicester LE1 4SE.
Telephone: 01926 332713 Email: secretary@royalaeroclub.org
www.royalaeroclub.org

LIST OF ABBREVIATIONS

(A)	Aircraft, when shown after PPL
AAC	Army Air Corps
ADF	Automatic Direction Finder
AEF	Air Experience Flight
AH	Artificial Horizon
AIS	Aeronautical Information Service
AME	Authorized Medical Examiner
AOPA	Aircraft Owners and Pilots Association
ASI	Air Speed Indicator
ATC	Air Traffic Control or Air Training Corps
ATPL	Airline Transport Pilot Licence
BAE	British Aerospace
CAA	Civil Aviation Authority
CAP	Civil Aviation Publication
CCF	Combined Cadet Force
CES	Cranwell Entry Standard
Cg	Centre of gravity
CPL	Commercial Pilot Licence
CRT	Cathode Ray Tube (display)
DE	Direct Entry (Army Air Corps)
DI	Directional Indicator
EASA	European Aviation Safety Agency
ECG	Electrocardiograph
EFIS	Electronic Flight Instrumentation System
FAA	Federal Aviation Administration
FAI	Fédération Aeronautique Internationale
FCL	Flight Crew Licensing
FI	Flying Instructor
FRTO	Flight Radiotelephony Operator
FTS	Flying Training School
(G)	Gliders, when shown after PPL
GFT	General Flight Test
GST	General Skill Test
(H)	Helicopters, when shown after PPL
IAT	International Air Tattoo
ICAO	International Civil Aviation Organization
IFR	Instrument Flight Rules
IMC	Instrument Meteorological Conditions
IR	Instrument Rating
JAA	Joint Aviation Authority
JAR	Joint Aviation Requirements
LAPL	Light Aircraft Pilot Licence
MCC	Multi-Crew Co-operation

ME	Multi-Engine
MoD	Ministry of Defence
NATS	National Air Traffic Services
NCO	Non-commissioned officer
NPPL	National Private Pilot Licence
NST	Navigation Skill Test
OASC	Officer and Aircrew Selection Centre
OCU	Operational Conversion Unit
PIC	Pilot-in-Command
PPL	Private Pilot Licence
QFE	'Q' Code for height above ground level
QNH	'Q' Code for height above sea level
RAeC	Royal Aero Club
RMAS	Royal Military Academy Sandhurst
RN(AS)	Royal Navy/Naval (Air Station)
RT	Radio Telephony
SEP	Single Engine Piston aircraft
SLMG	Self-Launching Motor Glider
SSC	Short Service Commission (Army officers)
SSEA	Simple Single Engine Aircraft
STOVL	Short Take-off/Vertical Landing
T&S	Turn & Slip Indicator
TWU	Tactical Weapons Unit
UAS	University Air Squadron
U/S	Under Supervision
VDU	Visual Display Unit
VGS	Volunteer Gliding School
VHF	Very High Frequency
VLJ	Very Light Jet
VOR	VHF Omni-directional Range
VR	Voluntary Reserve
VSI	Vertical Speed Indicator

INDEX

abbreviations, list of 152
Aeroprakt A22 Foxbat microlight
  55
Agusta A109 helicopter 95
ailerons 12, 13, 15
aircraft rating 36
air experience flight 23
airline transport pilot licence 62,
  65–72
  aeroplanes 65–69
  examinations 65, 68–69, 70–72
  experience required 66, 69–70
  'frozen' 62, 65, 66, 70, 76
  helicopters 69–72
  integrated course 66–69, 70–72
  medical requirements 65, 69
  modular course 69
  revalidation 69
  skill test 70
  validity 69
Air Training Corps 96–98
  contact details 146
  gliding schools 97
altimeter 16–17
airspeed indicator 16
armed forces careers offices 146
artificial horizon 17
ATR 72 airliner 65
authorized medical examiner 26
automatic direction finder 18
aviation related contact addresses
  150

BAE
  125 95
  146 95
  Hawk 85, 91, 93, 96, 101

Beechcraft
  King Air 60
  Super King Air 200 62, 91, 92
Boeing 747-400 68
Boeing Chinook helicopter 94, 95
Boeing/Westland Apache helicopter
  104, 105
brakes 14
British airlines contact addresses
  139
British Army 101–105
  aircrew selection 101–102
  contact details 146
  training 103–104

Canberra PR9 95
carburettor
  heat control 15
  icing 15
cathode-ray-tube displays 16
centre of gravity 11, 12
Cessna
  150 9, 20
  152 9–18, 24
  172 Skyhawk 25
  Aerobat 9, 20
  Citation Mustang 59
check ride 37
Civil Aviation Authority 20, 21,
  27, 33, 34, 45, 46, 51, 105
  approved overseas flight training
  schools 138
cockpit 13–14
  'glass' 16
commercial pilot courses 72–77
  integrated 72–76
  modular 76–77

training concessions for
experienced pilots 76
commercial pilot licence 57–83
aeroplanes 57–62
cost 73
examinations 58–59, 64
helicopters 62–65
hours credit for PPL holder 58
integrated course 58–59, 62–63
medical requirements 57, 62
modular course 59–60, 63–64
restrictions 57
skill test 59, 64
training abroad 80–81
contact names and addresses
106–151
aviation related 150
British airlines, scheduled, charter
and cargo operators 139
CAA approved overseas flight
training schools 138
military pilots 146
pilot publications and equipment
retailers 148
private, commercial and airline
pilots 145
professional pilot flight training
schools 137
UK private pilot licence training
schools 106
control
column 13
stick 11
surfaces 11–13
wheel 11, 13–14
yokes 13, 15
controls 14–16
engine 14–16
crew resource management training
61

de Havilland
Tiger Moth 9, 10
Twin Otter 60
Diamond DA40 53

differences training 37, 52
direction indicator 18
distance measuring equipment 31
dual-ignition system 16

electronic flight instrumentation
system 16
elevators 11, 12, 13, 14, 15
Embraer Bandeirante 60
Eurocopter EC135 73
Eurofighter Typhoon 91, 92, 93,
94
European Aviation Safety Agency
20, 45, 56

fin 11–12
first solo flight 30–31
flaps 12–13
flight crew licensing 20
flight instructor rating 77–80
course 78
experience required 77–78
funding 79–80
helicopters 79
removal of restriction 78–79
skill test 78
flight radiotelephony operator
licence 36
fuel
pump 14
selector 14

Gazelle helicopter 104
'glass cockpit' 16
Globemaster 96
Griffin helicopter 92, 93, 96
Grob
103 glider 97
109B self-launching motor glider
54, 97
115 Tutor 10, 86, 91, 97, 98,
100
ground training facilities 23

Harrier 91, 94, 99, 100–101

Hercules 95, 96
horizontal stabilizer 11

'idle cut-off' position 15
IMC rating 44–46
instructors 22–23
instrument
  flight rules 46
  rating 47–49, 60, 69, 72
instruments 16–18
  engine and system 17–18
  flight 16–17
  navigation 18
insurance 26

Joint Aviation Authority 20
Joint Aviation Requirements 20
'joystick' 13

King Air B200 92

light aircraft pilot licence 56
Lockheed Martin Joint Strike
  Fighter 99, 101
Luscombe Silvaire 43
Lynx helicopter 101, 103, 104

magnetic compass 18
magneto 16
  switch 16
medical certificate
  for NPPL 52
  JAR Class 1 26, 39, 57, 65, 69,
  72–73
  JAR Class 2 26, 39, 72
  validity 27, 52, 73
Merlin helicopter 95, 101
military pilot 84–105
mixture control 16
multi-crew co-operation training
  61–62, 65, 69

national pilots licensing group 51
national private pilot licence 19,
  50, 51–56, 86, 98

general skill test 54, 55
medical requirements 26, 52, 55
microlight course 54–56
ratings 51–52
restrictions 51–52, 56
revalidation 54, 56
SSEA/SLMG course 52–54
validity 54, 56
night qualification 43
Nimrod 93, 95, 96

personal flying log book 33
pilot publications and equipment
  retailers 148
  'pinch hitter's' course 50
Piper
  Cadet 9
  Cherokee (PA-28) 9, 11,13, 14
  Cherokee Six (PA-32) 35
  Seneca 58
  Tomahawk 9, 24
  Warrior 9, 10
'power lever' 14
primer 16
private pilot licence 19–50
  carriage of passengers 37
  certificate of test 36
  cost 24–25, 39–40
  course 28–36, 39
  examinations 33–34, 39
  flying abroad 37
  ground training 32–33
  helicopters 38–40
  medical requirements 26–28, 39
  restrictions 37
  revalidation 37
  skill test 32, 34–35
  training abroad 40–43
  training schools and clubs 106
  training for disabled 28
professional pilot flight training
  schools 137
Puma helicopter 95, 96

'Q' codes 16–17

QFE 16–17
QNH 16–17

'radials' 18
radio
 communications 18
 telephony 36
ratings 36, 51
 class 37
 flight instructor 77–80
 IMC 44–46
 instrument 47–49, 60, 69, 72
 multi-engine aircraft 46–47, 61,
 65, 69
 night 43
 revalidation 37, 46, 47
 type 37
 validity 37
Robin
 200 10
 400 10
Robinson R22/R44 helicopter 40
Royal Air Force 13, 84–98
 aircrew training 91–93
 contact details 146
 ranks 93–94
 selection of aircrew 89–91
 squadron service 94
Royal Navy 99–101
 contact details 146
 promotion 101
 selection of aircrew 100–101
 training 100–101
rudder 12, 13
 pedals 14, 15

safety pilot's course 50
Sea King helicopter 93, 95, 96,
 100, 101

Sentinel R1 94
Sentry AEW 94, 95
Short Tucano 85, 91, 92, 101
Slingsby Firefly 91, 92, 100, 104
Squirrel helicopter 92, 93, 101,
 104
starter switch 16

tail group 11–12
tailplane 11, 12
tanks (fuel) 14
Textron-Lycoming 0-235 10
throttle 14, 15
Tornado 90, 91, 93, 94, 95, 96
training organizations 21, 106
 how to choose 21–23
trial lessons 23–24
trim
 tab 11, 14
 wheel 14
Tristar 96
turn co-ordinator 17
turn-and-slip indicator 17
Tutor T1 92

University Air Squadrons 85–89
 contact details 146

VC10 96
vertical speed indicator 17
vertical stabilizer 11–12
very light jet 59
VHF direction finding 31
VHF omni-directional range 18,
 31
VHF radio transmitter 35

wings 12–13
wireless telegraphy 16